The
Happiness
Equation
W O R K S H O P

25 Deep Thoughts & Proven Methods for Catching & Keeping Happiness

+ + - -

by Shaun Roundy, MA
The University of Life

September 22, 2020 (updated 2023)
Orem, Utah

ISBN 978-1-893594-31-9

Chapter 1: Happiness Quotient	3
Chapter 2: Inform vs Transform	4
Chapter 3: Happiness, Defined	6
Chapter 4: Happiness Types	9
Chapter 5: Happiness Sources	12
Chapter 6: The Happiness Equation, Part One	14
Chapter 7: The Happiness Equation, Part Two	17
Chapter 8: Pay to Play	21
Chapter 9: Many Happy Returns	23
Chapter 10: Now & Later	26
Chapter 11: Pleasure	30
Chapter 12: Imagine Happiness	35
Chapter 13: Relief	37
Chapter 14: Laughter	41
Chapter 15: Humor	44
Chapter 16: Meaning	49
Chapter 17: Good Company	54
Chapter 18: Think Happy Thoughts	56
Chapter 19: Inches	59
Chapter 20: Enjoy Yourself	62
Chapter 21: Delusions of Grandeur	65
Chapter 22: Nature is Nurture	70
Chapter 23: Play	73
Chapter 24: Courage	77
Chapter 25: Judge and Jury	81
Chapter 26: The Narrow Now	85
Chapter 27: Live in the Past	90
Chapter 28: Clarity	94
Chapter 29: True Princess	97
Chapter 30: Get What You Give	101
To Be Continued...	105
More books by Shaun Roundy:	107
About the Author	124

Chapter 1: Happiness Quotient

Have you ever wondered why buffet lines always put the salad first? That's so you'll fill your plate before you get to the good stuff - the more expensive meats that the chef hopes to conserve until the last guest dishes up.

Similarly, the best part of life is happiness, but it often seems there's not much space for it after all those responsibilities you must attend to. Go to bed. Wake up. Cook, clean, study, work, fold laundry, floss, repeat.

Even if you had a large enough plate to fit everything on, you'd still have to address the inherently mysterious, unknown nature of nearly everything. Which dressing should you choose? Which side dish leads to the greatest satisfaction and the least suffering? Which school or job or vacation or friends or any number of other choices you must make as your life ticks steadily away?

Even after you've made your selections, sat down at the table, and lifted the first forkfull to your mouth, let's not forget unhealed wounds which force you to chew cautiously lest the former toothache return and make the meal impossible to enjoy.

Add to that worries about consuming too many calories or harmful chemicals, like spending too much money or enjoying too much time in the sun, and you may begin to wonder whether eating and living are even worth the effort.

Nobody told you exactly how you can live happily ever after - or rather, too many voices clamber for your attention, promising satisfaction in so many directions that you've left not quite knowing who to believe and which direction to take.

If you ever feel that way, then what you need is to increase your Happiness Quotient - your HQ, your understanding of exactly how happiness works and your ability to implement that knowledge, so you can fill your plate with healthy, effective attitudes and activities to make you feel good both in the moment and long into the future.

That's why we wrote this book for you - to explain how happiness works so effectively that you can not misunderstand and will never forget.

Chapter 2: Inform vs Transform

The Happiness Equation is designed to do more than merely *tell* you what happiness is and how to get it. It also guides you to make this journey personal by taking steps to *experience* these lessons for yourself.

If you have a foodie friend, you've probably endured their impassioned descriptions of the taste, texture, color, second taste, arrangement, and other details of whatever they ate for lunch. At worst, you may have found their obsession annoying. At best, it made you hungry to taste it for yourself.

We hope you don't merely learn valuable information from this book. We hope you don't only walk away wiser from having read it. Rather, we hope you try the strategies for yourself and taste the increased happiness as a result. We hope this experience changes you forever, making it impossible to revert to former, unhappier habits and perspectives.

That's why we include WORKSHOP sections with each chapter, which guide you to Ponder & Discuss (or journal, if you have no one discuss with) and Take Action, along with a few inspiring quotes ("In Other Words") to further clarify each lesson and embed them into your memory.

As an added bonus, deeper personal experience will increase your motivation to apply them again and again, making your efforts more effortless, and raising your happiness levels ever higher.

We'll make it as fun and easy as possible, but you may need to stretch your comfort zone now and then. Only then will you stop doing pretty much what you've always done, and be rewarded with pretty much the same level of happiness that you previously enjoyed.

The chapters themselves are only a menu. If you hope to improve your circumstances and enjoy greater life satisfaction, you must apply the recipes in the real world.

Ponder & Discuss

1. How much do you already know about how happiness works? Give a few examples.
2. How much does that knowledge translate into action, and how much does that action result in increased happiness?
3. What insurmountable obstacles to happiness are you

familiar with, or at least which impediments make happiness especially difficult for you? What solutions can you imagine that might help the situation?

Take Action

1. Actually discuss one of those three questions with someone. Pose the question casually, if you like, listen to how others respond, and (probably) surprise yourself at how willing people are to share their opinions on such universally-interesting topics.

    Note that you'll find most people much more willing to speak with you when you do more asking and listening than talking. Then write a paragraph about what you learned from the conversation.

In Other Words

"The happiest people you will ever see are those who are adaptable to change." - Robert Puff

"Wisdom literature points you in a general direction, but you will not gain the wisdom until you have walked the path yourself." – Shaun Roundy

"You must believe in the possibility of happiness in order to be happy." – Leo Tolstoy

Chapter 3: Happiness, Defined

As it turns out, you can define happiness in two ways - very specifically, or very generally, and both definitions have their benefits.

When I was in high school and college, I dated very "generally." If I met someone who seemed fun and attractive, I would ask her out, and we'd usually get along just fine. If we got along well enough, then we'd date more seriously, and while this was also nice, it got in the way of dating more "specifically," because when I met someone who I was *really* drawn to, I was already "taken" and less free to pursue her. Sometimes it's worth being picky.

But if you're too picky, you could miss out on a lot of grand learning experiences while waiting for your one and only, or whatever you're hoping to gain, and you risk the possibility that it will never arrive.

When it comes to defining and pursuing happiness, which approach is best? That question can not be answered absolutely, because it depends on so many factors. So let's explore the best of both worlds.

This chapter will provide the broadest-possible, all-encompassing definition of happiness in order to open the door and invite every type of positive vibe into your life, and Chapter 4 will introduce dozens of distinct, specific happiness types for you to pursue. Later chapters will reveal the pros and cons of each option.

On one hand, happiness needs no definition. After all, you know it when you feel it.

Then again, maybe it does need a clear definition, because merely recognizing an ice cream cone or happy ending or Lamborghini does not make them yours, and what good are such things if you don't get to enjoy them?

Defining things gives you power over them. It creates a place in your brain for their concept to exist, and the more clearly an idea exists in your mind, the more likely it will show up in your physical reality, as well.

That's because ideas shape behavior, and behavior shapes circumstances more than any other factor.

In general terms, happiness simply means feeling good, or, to put it more precisely:

Happiness is Experiencing Enjoyable Emotional States

With a working definition of happiness now in place, the "secret" to happiness becomes blatantly obvious: think and do and have and be the things that put you into that state and keep you there.

This is what you're after, after all. You want to feel good.

Ideally, you'd like that to happen effortlessly, instantly, and permanently, but is that possible? In some cases, and to varying degrees...*yes!* Absolutely.

In other ways, absolutely not, but that doesn't necessarily make the more difficult, time-consuming methods less important. You'll have to decide for yourself.

You simply need to know proven ways to make happiness happen and then follow through until you master each perspective and skill, and that's exactly what this book guides you through.

Understanding what happiness means and how to get it is only half the battle. Make the decision right now that as you learn how to be happier, you will act on that knowledge and reap its rewards.

Ponder & Discuss

1. Raise your awareness of happiness in your life by listing at least 5 recent enjoyable emotional states which you have experienced.

   You may define "recent" however you like, and they don't each have to be unique, but do see how many different types or flavors of happiness (enjoyable emotional states) you can list, such as fun, excitement, contentment, enjoyment, purpose and satisfaction, humor and mirth, and so forth. Don't just write "fun," "excitement," and so forth, but list *specific* instances of them, like "I saw a beautiful sunset and felt peaceful," or "I saw a funny bumper sticker and laughed," or "Jane and I jumped from a hot air balloon and parachuted to a secluded island for the weekend together, and I felt excited and loved."

2. For extra credit, share some of your list on social media or discuss it with a friend or study partner for this course. If

you don't have a study partner, try inviting someone who responds well to your comments.

For example, you could write, "I have a homework assignment from the University of Life to share and discuss an enjoyable emotional experience, and last weekend I went for a pleasant walk in the woods. Does anybody else make time for that sort of thing? What do you like about it?"

Take Action

3. Do something that puts you in an enjoyable emotional state, then write a paragraph about how much effort it took, how long the happiness lasted, and why it made you happy.
It's okay if you don't yet understand everything perfectly - the primary point is to ask yourself these questions, which increases your overall awareness and prepares your mind for upcoming lessons.

In Other Words

"Words are, of course, the most powerful drug used by mankind." – Rudyard Kipling

"No matter what people will tell you, words and ideas can change the world." – Robin Williams

"Words are where most change begins." – Brandon Sanderson

"There are times when the world is rearranging itself, and at times like that, the right words can change the world." – Orson Scott Card

Chapter 4: Happiness Types

My high school friend Doug's father owned the local Super Taco restaurant, and being obnoxious teens, we sometimes pulled up to the drive through and ordered a taco.

"What kind do you want?" the employee would ask.

"What kinds do you have?" we would ask in return. Once they rattled off the dozen or so options, we would say, "Nevermind. Give me a burrito."

The point is, if you simply say "Give me some happiness!", that's not very specific, which makes your order difficult to fulfill. After all, there are so many types of happiness to choose from, and so many sources through which to generate it.

It's like love. Everyone assumes that whatever scraps and tidbits of knowledge they happen to understand about love is pretty well all there is to know.

Then they wait or wander around wishing for it to happen to them, while if they only understood love a little bit more, they would know precisely how to go out and make it happen.

Likewise, most people have a general understanding of what happiness means with vague ideas about how to get it, which often results in rather random efforts and only inconsistent or mediocre returns.

If only they could define happiness as clearly as they design their morning venti, 7-pump vanilla soy, 12-scoop matcha, 182-degree, no-foam, green-tea latte at Starbucks! Then they could ask for exactly what type of happiness they want, which would make them more likely to get it.

Happiness is notoriously difficult to precisely define because it encompasses so many different - and often *very* different - states of mind.

It's like the word "dog," which describes everything from deer-sized Great Danes, to tiny creatures which fit in your pocket, and hundreds of breeds in between; or ice cream, which you can enjoy in dozens of different flavors to match your unique and variable preferences.

The Greeks defined multiple types or categories of happiness (primarily eudaimonia, which translates roughly to meaningful satisfaction and well-being, and hedonia, which refers to various types of pleasure).

Positive psychology categorizes happiness in slightly different ways: the pleasant life (similar to hedonism); flow or the engaged life; and the meaningful life (similar to eudaimonia).

You can find many other lists of happiness types online, which usually consist of relatively random groups of enjoyable emotional states, or the objects and activities which generate those states.

We strongly agree with psychology professor Todd Kashdan, who writes, "Can we please stop the rat-race between abstract, wastebasket terms? [Like arguing over the exact definition of eudaimonia.] There is a better approach. Learn about where you and others fall on different dimensions. With greater precision in our language and measures, we can better improve our quality of life" [paraphrased].

By delving deeper into specific types of happiness and the thoughts and actions which produce them, we'll change the discussion from pure abstraction to practical, concrete application, which will yield far more useful results.

Examples of happiness types we'll explore throughout this series include:

Peace	Fun	Relief	Excitement
Pleasure	Curiosity	Growth	Love
Security	Connection	Laughter	Beauty
Meaning	Health	Engagement	Perspective
Freedom	Clarity	Pride	Hope
Courage	Awe	Inspiration	Flow
Success	Wellness	Care-freeness	Spirituality

There's no use arguing which happiness types are best and which ones everyone in the world should seek first. Life is a smorgasbord and you are free to pick and choose as many happiness types as you like - but you should understand your choices, along with their costs and consequences, before spending your whole life always choosing the same menu item.

Some happiness types are light and simple, while others are complex and intricate.

Some are readily available and easily obtained, while others may require significant effort and investment, at least at first.

Some are more surfacy and fleeting, while others reach all the way into your core and may linger much longer, possibly permanently altering the way you view yourself and the wide world around you, turning you into a naturally happier individual.

Some are healthy, promoting your ongoing well-being, while others come at the cost of future peace and prosperity.

As you explore the dozens of happiness sources throughout this book and the types of happiness they produce, ask yourself which types you prefer and how much time and effort you're willing to expend to enjoy each one more often and more thoroughly.

Me? I'd be more than happy to pay $7 for a cup of vanilla bean peace, pleasure, fun, growth, awe, love, connection, success on my way to work each morning.

WORKSHOP

Ponder & Discuss

1. When was the last time you experienced each type of happiness listed above?
2. What are the pros and cons of each type?
3. Is there a best type? Why or why not?
4. Circle the happiness types that you cherish most from the above list (or add your own).
5. For extra credit, record two numbers next to your favorites - first, a number from 1 to 10 to show how much you currently have of each one, then another number to show how much you'd *like* to have.

    If you have 7 peace and that's good enough, write 7/7. If you have 2 love but want 8, write 2/8. This helps clarify your goals and directs what to watch for in upcoming chapters.

Take Action

1. Do something which generates multiple happiness types at the same time - like something fun and meaningful, or interesting and beautiful, or courageous and connecting, then write a paragraph about how different happiness types affect and enhance each other.

In Other Words

"It doesn't matter what you do on the outside as long as you're dancing on the inside." – Shaun Roundy

Chapter 5: Happiness Sources

I had run a few miles up a mountain trail one summer morning, and found myself thirsty and hot. But rather than return to civilization with its drinking fountains and air conditioning, I kept going, because I knew what I would find in the next meadow.

A small, white, plastic pipe poked out of the ground there, and cool, clear spring water ran from it. I splashed the water over my face and shoulders, cupped my hands and drank my fill, then continued running up the narrow canyon.

The trees along the trail crowded in and stilled the air, and I soon found myself dripping with sweat again, but once I reached the top of the canyon, the trees opened into another small meadow, and a cool breeze caressed my bare skin and refreshed me all over again.

For every type of happiness (in this example, you could call it refreshment, or the broader term, pleasure), there are thousands of sources to help you experience it.

I could have stayed home and enjoyed a drink of cold water, though the refreshment wouldn't have felt nearly as pleasant since I wouldn't have craved it as much before quenching my thirst.

I could have driven to the river and dived in, though it ran cold with snowmelt from higher in the mountains, and that may have proven more "refreshing" than I wanted.

It helps to stay aware of all the opportunities to generate happiness that surround you so you don't end up waiting for one that never pans out, while missing out on more productive options.

Common happiness sources include:

Humor	Fun activities	Food	Freedom
Money	Success	Exotic vacation	Romance
Laughter	Bike ride	Massage	Accomplishment
Health	Music	Praise	Sleeping in
Mastery	Spirituality	Friendship	Winning the lottery

Any time you wish to experience happiness, all you need is to select a happiness source and put it into play.

The source does not always guarantee happiness, but without a source to kick things off, happiness has no way to reach you. Without a happiness source, there can be no happiness.

If one source fails you this time around, simply try out another.

Once we finish explaining a few more key concepts, most of this book will present various happiness sources for you to practice and learn.

WORKSHOP

Ponder & Discuss

1. Which happiness sources do you judge as superior or inferior to others? What makes them better or worse?
2. Which happiness sources are the easiest?
3. Which are most difficult?
4. Which are most worthwhile? Why?
5. Which happiness sources do you have plenty of, and which would you like to have more of?

Take Action

1. Do something that will make you feel happy, and observe the happy feelings as they happen, then write a paragraph describing your experience.
   For example: "I told Holly that I love and appreciate her, and I saw her eyes light up as little as she smiled in return. I noticed my love for her increase, and I felt proud of her and grateful to have her in my life."

In Other Words

"It is not easy to find happiness in ourselves and it is not possible to find it elsewhere." – Anges Repplier

"All the happiness there is in this world comes from thinking about others, and all the suffering comes from preoccupation with yourself." – Shantideva

"The essentials for happiness are: something to do, someone to love, and something to hope for." – Joseph Addison

"Happiness comes from moving toward something." – Michael J. Sullivan

Chapter 6: The Happiness Equation, Part One

The "secret" to happiness is hardly a secret. If happiness means feeling good, then all you need is to do what makes you feel good.

With thousands of ways to feel good always within reach, you can simplify this concept down to the following equation:

Plus plus. The first half of the Happiness Equation simply advises you to increase the positives in your life - get more of them. Do, think, have and be what makes you happy more often and more intensely.

Get more sleep. Buy a new toy and use it often. Call an old friend and get reacquainted. Clean the bathroom. While you're there, look in the mirror and see the good, not the bad, in your reflection. Fall in love. Make an extra donation to your retirement account, or to your favorite charitable cause.

Plus plus also encourages you to derive more happiness from the sources which already exist around you.

Visit a nearby park for lunch and pay more attention to the trees, the sun and shadows, and to the happy people relaxing there.

See the good in your family and neighbors, and forgive and forget their minor shortcomings, as well as your own.

Glance up at the sky or the trees or buildings on your drive home and let their rich colors or interesting geometries seep deeply into your soul. Turn on some music if that helps, or roll down the window and let the wind blow through your hair.

Put away the laundry hanging on your treadmill and run a few laps, paying attention to how it makes your lungs and legs feel more active and alive. Hurry up, before you change your mind!

You already plus plus naturally, instinctively, reaching for a snack when you feel hungry or stressed, reaching out to friends or your phone when you feel bored, and filling evenings and weekends with entertainment.

But consciously plus plussing empowers you to do so even more intelligently, less haphazardly, and thus raise your permanent happiness state to the next level.

This formula appears impossibly simple, yet it also paints a perfectly clear path forward. There can be no other formula for adding happiness to your life, because this simple equation encompasses all happiness sources!

"What about finding my soulmate and falling in love?" you may ask, "wouldn't that make me happier than your simple happiness equation?"

Well, that's already included.

"What about winning the lottery?"

That's covered, too.

"What about flossing more regularly, or getting in shape, or discovering a time machine, or gaining super powers like learning how to fly?"

Like I said, plus plus includes every possible way to become happier.

If you're exceptionally bright, you may have already caught the vision of how dramatically these two little crosses are about to change your life for the better, and maybe you've already written them on the back of your hand as a reminder, or you're looking for your car keys so you can drive down to the tattoo parlor to permanently inscribe your new life motto on your shoulder: "Plus Plus, Baby!"

Of course there are important nuances to consider, additional rules and insights to guide you, and hundreds of variables for applying this formula, and we'll explain those points in upcoming chapters.

Ponder & Discuss

1. Which readily available happiness sources are currently under-utilized in your life? How and when could you make better use of them?
2. Which happiness sources have you never tried, but always wanted to?
3. What would happen to your happiness levels if you tried out one new happiness source to every day, or every week? How might that change the way you see yourself and the way others think of you?

Take Action

1. Do something you listed for question 1 or 2, then write a paragraph exploring how glad you are that you did it, and whether you'd like to do it more often?
2. Try a brand-new happiness source which you've never experienced before. For example, a desert you've heard others talk about, or writing a gratitude letter to someone who made a valuable contribution to your life, then record the way it influenced your happiness level.

In Other Words

"A man is relieved and gay when he has put his heart into his work and done his best, but what he has said or done otherwise shall give him no peace." – Ralph Waldo Emerson

"Well done is better than well said." - Benjamin Franklin

"Nothing great or new can be done without enthusiasm. Enthusiasm is the fly-wheel which carries your saw through the knots in the log." – Harvey Cushing

"In vain do they talk of happiness who never subdued an impulse in obedience to a principle. He who never sacrificed a present to a future good, or a personal to a general one, can speak of happiness only as the blind do of colors." – Horace Mann

"Much happiness is overlooked because it doesn't cost anything." – Arthur Schopenhauer

Chapter 7: The Happiness Equation, Part Two

With a business trip scheduled in Florida on January 5, I decided to fly out on December 26, buy a kayak on Craigslist, and paddle alone for 120 miles through Rookery Bay, the Ten Thousand Islands, and Everglades National Park. Just me and the dolphins and sharks, turtles and crocodiles.

On the 27th, I woke up in paradise, surrounded by the calming sound of gentle waves washing up a white-sand beach backed by mangroves. I crawled from the tent and ate breakfast, then broke camp and paddled south. The December weather was clear and warm, and my mood was high, despite the daunting ordeal that lay before me.

Did you know that happiness is the natural state of being alive? With your basic needs met and no immediate threats, you ought to be able to relax and enjoy whatever opportunities each day offers. People don't need that many plusses or excuses to feel happy.

I paddled all day long, pausing for lunch on Marco Island, then said goodbye to my last view of civilization for the next eight days as I continued south, then east, catching the rising tide flowing toward the day's goal - Coon Key, the tiny island where I would sleep on the beach.

After covering 21 miles, I arrived at just after sunset. As I dragged the boat up the beach above the high tide line, I realized that the hull had a small hole, and at least ten gallons of water had leaked inside the kayak.

The water inside the boat reduced its flotation by over 80 pounds, which made it sink a few inches deeper into the ocean, and every yard of progress required me to push against that much more resistance.

I tried to find and patch the hole with duct tape, with only moderate success, so for the next seven days, I would stop on an island or chickee once or twice during the day to drain the water, which made paddling for the next hundred miles considerably easier.

Similarly, feeling happy is often less about doing what makes you feel good, and more about removing the influences that drag you down, that hold you back and limit your progress and happiness.

Thus, the second half of the Happiness Equation addresses an equally important path to happiness:

$$- \; -$$

Minus minus. This directs you to Identify, remove, or at least diminish the influence of happiness detractors such as:

Stress	Fear	Overwhelm	Loneliness
Frustration	Anxiety	Doubt	Depression
Pessimism	Grief	Despair	Scarcity

and the many other antonyms of happiness.

"Ha!" you may respond. "Easier said than done!"

True, but that's what this *Live Your Best Life* book series is for, to teach you easy and effective ways to make that happen.

Sometimes you'll do this by changing your environment. Sometimes you'll change the way you *react* to your environment. And sometimes it all happens on the inside, in the way you manage your health, thoughts and feelings.

You may never succeed at eliminating all negatives, but this series will teach you many concrete steps to decrease how strongly they influence your mood, perspective and performance.

The complete Happiness Equation reads:

$$++, \; - \; -$$

Plus plus, minus minus. More good, less bad.

Read on to continue increasing lift and decreasing drag to keep you floating as high as possible through life's endless periods of calm and storm.

Ponder & Discuss

1. List the top three factors which diminish your happiness. Don't go the extra mile, stop at three. Don't focus on them too much, which could spread their dark shadow further.
2. How could you remove or reduce these negatives? If you can't change them, how could you learn to let them affect you less?
3. Discuss one or two of these with someone you trust. Someone who cares about you. Or a stranger, if you like. You don't need to fix them, and you don't need to get all worked up and sad or angry about them. Just test your ability to open up and share your burdens honestly, and maybe find some support.
If you don't want sympathy or solutions, go ahead and mention that up front, but if your listener goes there anyway, be patient with them or change the subject.

Take Action

1. If one of your minuses is something you can take action on - like finishing a stressful assignment or a home improvement project you've put off for too long, or reconciling with a friend or family member - then do something about it today. You don't need to finish, just begin, with the assurance that even baby steps will eventually bring you to the finish line.
2. If one of your minuses is caused by your own negative thinking habits, then vow to change those thoughts, even if you don't yet know how to make that happen. Speak your commitment out loud so your brain will know that you mean it.

In Other Words

"Happiness is easy. It is letting go of unhappiness that is hard."– Hugh Prather

"Westerners mistakenly think that nirvana is what arrives when all your woe is behind you and you have only bliss to look forward to, but that would not be nirvana because your bliss in the present would always be shadowed by the [woe] from the past. Nirvana is what you arrive at when you have only bliss to look forward to and find in what looked like sorrows, the seedlings of your joy." – Andrew Solomon

"Perhaps the surest cure for discouragement is to do something about your situation with the certainty that action changes everything." – Shaun Roundy

"The most beautiful people we have known are those who have known defeat, known suffering, known struggle, known loss, and have found their way out of the depths. These persons have an appreciation, a sensitivity and an understanding of life that fills them with compassions, gentleness, and a deep loving concern. Beautiful people do not just happen." – Elizabeth Kubler-Ross

"Your task is not to seek for love, but merely to seek and find all the barriers within yourself that you have built against it." – Rumi

Chapter 8: Pay to Play

Happiness always comes at a cost, just like everything else in this world.

If you want to enjoy an ice cream cone or jelly-filled donut, you must invest between fifty cents and a few dollars.

If you want flat abs, it'll cost you thousands of crunches, and you'll have to deny yourself some of those ice cream cones and donuts.

If you want to feel happy, you must think happy thoughts, or take a walk, listen to something funny, notice something beautiful, do something meaningful, put in the effort to generate happiness from thin air, or pay whatever other cost your brain requires to ignite a spark of joy.

The next two chapters explain crucial considerations as you calculate the cost and rewards of each happiness type and source.

Ponder & Discuss

1. How comfortable do you feel with the idea of investing effort to get what you want?
2. How much do your expectations of success or failure influence your willingness to try something new?
3. Describe several instances when your efforts to experience happiness succeeded or failed. What might have made them more successful? What will you do differently next time around?

Take Action

1. Pick something you often do half-heartedly and do it with gusto and enthusiasm once or twice. Notice what difference that makes. Discuss (or journal about) whether you should consider paying more into life more often in order to get more back from it.

In Other Words

"Everyone is trying to accomplish something big, not realizing that life is made up of little things." – Frank A Clark

"It is the feeling of exerting effort that exhilarates us, as a grasshopper is exhilarated by jumping. A hard job, full of impediments, is thus more satisfying than an easy job." – H L Mencken

"I would rather be ashes than dust! I would rather that my spark should burn out in a brilliant blaze than it should be stifled by dryrot. I would rather be a superb meteor, every atom of me in magnificent glow, than a sleepy and permanent planet. The proper function of man is to live, not to exist. I shall not waste my days in trying to prolong them. I shall use my time." – Jack London

"A great deal of talent is lost in the world for want of a little courage. Every day sends to their graves men whom timidity prevented from making a first effort; who, if they could have been induced to begin, would in all probability have gone great lengths." – Sidney Smith

"If you want truly to understand something, try to change it." – Kurt Lewin

"Life is arranged against us. We're all yearning for a wedge of sky, aren't we? I suspect God plants these yearnings in us so we'll at least try and change the course of things. We must try, that's all." – Sue Monk Kidd

Chapter 9: Many Happy Returns

My high school band spent a night in Las Vegas on our way to a California competition (where, incidentally, we brought home a trophy taller than most of the flute players).

Todd sneaked out of the hotel late at night, evaded security in the casino, and tried his luck at the slot machines. When he returned to our room after 3 a.m., he gleefully reported that he had won fifty-seven dollars! That was a lot of money to a high school kid, so you can imagine that he was pretty excited.

Dubious, I asked how much he spent.

"Seventy."

That's what I thought. He hadn't really won a cent, but lost thirteen bucks.

Many happiness chasers make the same mistake. They try their best to do what they believe makes them happy, when in reality, the costs are higher and/or the returns lower than they perceive. They would be wise to quit before they get further behind, or at least diversify their portfolio by trying out some new investments.

Shopaholics and other addicts serve as the perfect example. Their temporary fix provides a certain rush or relief, but they soon come down and find themselves even deeper in debt and despair, which are the very conditions they sought to escape in the first place.

Before you pay whatever price a particular happiness source requires, it may be wise to consider the trade-offs. Are the returns worth whatever money, effort, time, or attention you paid?

Not all sources of happiness are created equal. Ideal happiness investments have small costs and large pay outs, though some happiness returns are worthwhile even when they require years of struggle and agonizing discomfort.

Some obvious cost and reward pairs include:

- Going to work or school. You put in your time and effort and receive a paycheck or a grade (and, eventually, a degree) in return.
- Exercise and eating healthy takes time and possibly some discomfort, but you look and feel better afterward.
- Chasing your dreams may require you to step out of your comfort zone, and you do so with the hope and expectation that the rewards will make all the discomfort worth it.
- Being social, if you're an extrovert, may require no

disagreeable costs, yet at the very least you must forfeit other ways you might have spent that time.

You can double check your return on investment by plotting them on the Happiness ROI (Return On Investment) graph. On the X axis, measure the happiness gained, and on the Y axis, measure the cost paid.

For example, if you really love ice cream cones and they cost only $3, then your chart may look something like this:

This is an ideal type of happiness source to invest in, with low costs and high rewards.

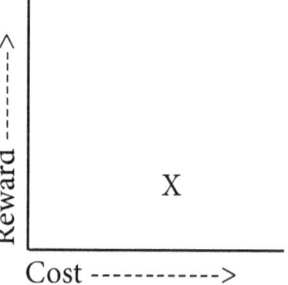

If you love buying expensive shoes but rarely wear and enjoy them (because you have *so many* to choose from!), your chart may look like this for the next pair you purchase:

I joined band in junior high so mom would let me quit piano lessons. I still had to practice, which didn't excite me, but the rewards came when we played well together, took second place in the competition, and enjoyed each others' company and friendship. The costs felt somewhat high, but the reward was even greater. In the final tally, I consider it an extremely worthwhile investment.

The choice of which costs to pay is up to you. Just make sure to double check now and then that you're spending your time and efforts wisely.

Ponder & Discuss

1. From which sources do you most often seek happiness? What are their costs?
2. What are their returns? How much happiness do those sources generate?
3. Do you consider them good investments? Or might you earn better returns and rewards elsewhere?

Take Action

1. Try out a new happiness investment strategy. Do something a little harder or easier than usual, then write a paragraph about whether or not it was worth the time and effort. For example: "I hate exercise, but I went for a walk anyway. I felt surprised at how nice it felt to get outside and breathe some fresh air, and should probably do so more often." Or: "Rather than just thinking about asking Laura out, I actually called and asked. She said no, but I felt proud of myself for at least trying! Was it worth it? Sure. And I learned to not waste so much time daydreaming about a girl before finding out whether those dreams have any chance of coming true."

In Other Words

"The chief cause of failure and unhappiness is trading what we want most for what we want in the moment." – Bertrand Russell

"The most successful people are those who are good at plan B." – James Yorke

"The secret of success is learning how to use pain and pleasure instead of having pain and pleasure use you. If you do that, you're in control of your life. If you don't, life controls you." – Tony Robbins

"Work is life. Love of work is success." – Shaun Roundy

Chapter 10: Now & Later

Across the street from my high school was a Hostess thriftshop which sold pastries which had recently passed their expiration date. I often had a box of almost-fresh, powdered, jelly-filled donuts stashed in my locker, which I generously shared with friends.

One day I tallied all the checks I had written for donuts over the past month or two, and it added up to $300.

I didn't change my spending habits, however, until I noticed that a best friend's little brother Lee had recently bought cross country skis and a motorcycle.

That's when it occurred to me that I could enjoy much longer-lasting satisfaction if I saved my pennies for more durable goods instead of immediate but fleeting pleasures to rot my teeth.

Use the Cost-and-Reward-Over-Time graph to visually measure the benefits of each course of action:

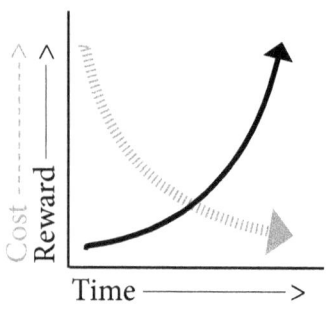

In this example, note that the cost decreases over time, while the reward increases.

This is like buying a pair of cross country skis. Once you've worked, saved your money, and paid for them, the only remaining costs are time, effort, and enduring some cold weather, while the reward of enjoying the beautiful winter wonderland and escaping cabin fever may last for as long as snow covers the ground.

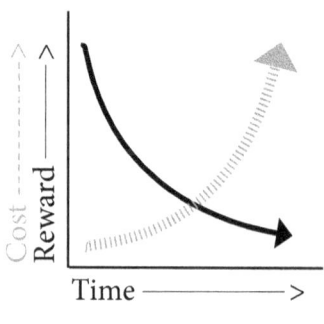

In this example, costs rise over time, while rewards rapidly diminish.

This aptly describes the type-two diabetes I may have developed if I had continued consuming as much sugar as I did as a teenager.

What about you? Are you a "play now, pay later" kind of person? Do you live for the moment and deal with the consequences later?

Would you proudly wear a t-shirt

with this Bible verse on it?

> "A man hath no better thing under the sun, than to eat, and to drink, and to be merry."
> - Ecclesiastes 8:15

Or do you take the long view and wisely delay gratification, willingly enduring present discomfort with the promise of future happiness?

> "A moment on the lips, forever on the hips." -
> Dieters' Creedo

All happiness has both costs and rewards, and the timing of those elements is worth considering. How can you decide which is better?

Immediate costs and rewards are a lot easier to believe in than those in the distant, uncertain future, but the way you behave today *creates* that future, and future rewards often prove more durable and deeply satisfying.

A glance at your monthly credit card statement may reveal something about your happiness-payment-plan preferences. Have you purchased things that you can't really afford, willingly paying additional interest until you somehow pay it off (or declare bankruptcy)?

Or do you live sufficiently within your means that you repay the entire balance each month, and thus avoid additional cost?

In reality, it's not an either/or question. You can play and pay both ways.

Enjoying happiness now is valuable because, among other things, it can shape your perception of life as a happy experience and transform you into a happier person for the future. It can generate memories for you to reflect on and smile about for years to come.

If you set aside all present happiness, saving all enjoyment to savor in the future, you may get there only to discover that it took much longer than you anticipated to arrive, and when you look back on your life, you may wish you had enjoyed your months and years of brief moments strung together end-to-end more often.

But ignoring the costs altogether, procrastinating necessary discomfort, and selling out future happiness because you don't feel like thinking about the future is a fool's errand.

The pain that you heap upon your future self may become unavoidable, and in the depths of your regret, in your wisdom-gained-too-late, you may wish for a fairy godmother to let you go back and do it all over.

In the end, planning your happiness strategy is an imperfect science at best, because you can't precisely predict what all the costs and rewards of your actions will be, so you'll have to take your best guess and move forward bravely into the unknown.

The important point of this chapter is that you at least pause to consider the timing of the costs and rewards of your choices, that you sample your options in your imagination to determine what works, and how well, before you step on the gas and set your course one way or the other.

Your Happiness Quotient will grow as you learn to play both ways - sometimes it's worth being the fool who rushes in, being the early bird who gets the worm, and other times it's best to hesitate, to calculate costs and rewards, both immediate and long-term, and not charge headlong toward every immediate pleasure that blips onto your radar.

WORKSHOP

Ponder & Discuss

1. List at least three happiness sources which match this graph, with higher initial costs but increasing rewards as time goes by.

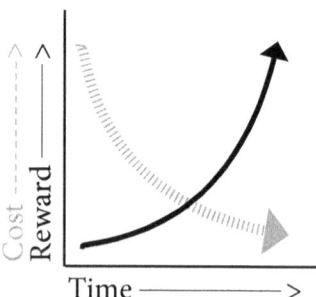

2. List three different happiness types or sources which deliver immediate returns at low cost, but whose rewards diminish

as costs grow.

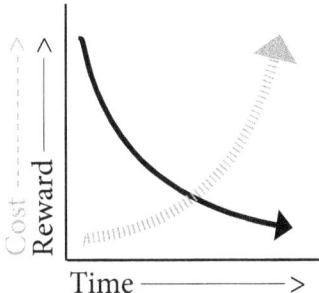

3. List at least three of your favorite happiness sources and draw a Happiness ROI graph for each one, showing their costs and rewards over time.
4. Review your graphs and look for trends. Do you find that you typically aim for immediate rewards, or do you tend to delay gratification?
Do the trends suggest that you ought to pursue some different types of happiness sources, aim for greater variety and diversify your portfolio, to enjoy the present more often, or invest more in future happiness?

Take Action

1. Do something to generate immediate happiness, and something else which will bring delayed happiness, then write a paragraph about which one you prefer, and explain why.

In Other Words

"That which is bitter to endure may be sweet to remember." – Thomas Fuller

"If we are ever in doubt what to do, it is a good rule to ask ourselves what we shall wish on the morrow that we had done." – Sir John Lubbock

Chapter 11: Pleasure

When my friend Dan bought a half-million-dollar sailboat in Venezuela and asked who would help him sail it home, I replied with a smile, "A friend in need is a friend indeed!"

I bought a one-way ticket to Aruba and only wore shoes three times for the next five weeks and 2,500 miles of ocean and island.

We first spent five days sailing 600 miles to Panama, then retreated to the San Blas islands to wait for our transit date through the Canal.

After anchoring our sailboat at a small, white-sand island covered in palm trees, the local residents paddled out to meet us in dugout canoes to sell beaded necklaces, intricately sewn applique designs, and food, in the form of delicious breadsticks and a large crab and lobster.

We counted our spending money, negotiated prices, tried to make the children smile, and purchased some of each item.

We were lucky to have David aboard, an accomplished chef, and later that night, we sat at a table on deck below a full moon and feasted.

The crabs were so large that we couldn't break them open with crab crackers, so Captain Dan went below and returned with channel locks - strong pliers from the tool kit with plenty of leverage, and that did the trick, cracking the tough shell open and revealing the delicacy hidden within.

With my fork, I pulled a large piece of tender, white crab meat from its shell, dipped it in a small cup of melted garlic butter, then opened my hungry mouth and set it on my tongue.

"Mmmmm!" I said, closing my eyes for a moment. "This is the best food I've ever tasted!" I'm not a big foodie, and I almost never take photos of what I'm eating to post on social media, but this... this caught my attention! I would not soon forget.

I sipped my bottle of Fanta de Piña in the bright moonlight and couldn't help but smile.

Pleasure is, by definition, pleasant, which, along with its easy accessibility, makes it one of the world's all-time-favorite sources of happiness. It may excite or relax you. It may quench an appetite or scratch an itch you didn't know you had.

On the other hand, You're probably old enough to have learned by experience that although pleasure may generate a sizeable and immediate happiness boost, it can also incur significant costs.

Eat too much and you'll feel sick now and gain weight later. Sleep in every morning and you'll fail your classes or get fired from your job. Ignore the laundry and dishes and other chores while playing endless video games and you'll find yourself living in a stinky, depressing pig sty.

For better or worse, pleasure suffers from diminishing returns -

we find the first sip of cool water indescribably refreshing, and the first bite of dessert tastes heavenly, but once your appetite gets sated, the added benefit of another sip or another bite grows ever smaller and more forgettable.

Living for pleasure is called Hedonism, and it's well known as one of the most surface types of happiness. Compared to other, deeper, more spiritual layers of existence, and especially in the absence of those others, it grows hollow and unsatisfying.

Those foolish enough (or fooled enough, by every company trying desperately to sell you their product by evoking the name of happiness) to put all their eggs in this basket, seeking endless pleasure to escape suffering and growth, may discover another serious danger of the pursuit of pleasure.

Pleasure releases the neurotransmitter dopamine, and while dopamine offers multiple benefits - including motivation and enhanced learning, too much of it reduces the number of serotonin receptors, which makes serotonin's more enduring contentment-style happiness become ever more elusive, if not impossible.

The downward cycle gains momentum as lower serotonin levels result in more dopamine, which prompts increasingly impulsive behavior. If you can't control your impulses, like dangerously checking your phone for social media messages while driving, you may already be suffering from this effect. You may be speeding your way toward addiction, depression, and other serious consequences.

But just because pleasure can be risky doesn't mean you should avoid it altogether.

You may argue that pleasure isn't actually happiness, that it's more of an enjoyable physical sensation than emotion, but remember, we cast a wide net, choosing a broad definition of happiness in order to catch every possible option to help you feel good, and a pleasant sensory experience may be just what you need to boost your mood momentarily and improve your perspective.

Rocking lazily back and forth as a hammock holds you in its gentle embrace, or something as simple and strangely satisfying as a sneeze might be the most rewarding way you can spend the next moment or two of your day.

Common sources of pleasure include

Touch	Smell	Motion	Sleep
Music	Warmth	Coolness	Sex

If we were capable of experiencing pleasure continuously, and if that were enough to keep us permanently happy, then I'm sure we'd all be perfectly satisfied to stop right there.

But alone will not keep you happy, as you now understand, so as you plan your personal happiness strategy, make sure to stock up on other happiness types as well.

Ponder & Discuss

1. List five of your favorite pleasures.
2. How recently and how often do you enjoy them? Why not more?
3. Draw a Happiness Reward and Happiness Cost graph for each of those five (you may draw a simple dot, as demonstrated in chapter 9, or lines to demonstrate rewards and costs over time, as in chapter 10).
4. Discuss one or two of these with someone, and find out what they enjoy and why.

Take Action

1. Schedule time for one of your favorite pleasures right now (or enjoy it immediately!). Afterward, write a paragraph about how it affected your happiness.

In Other Words

"Do not ask your children to strive for extraordinary lives. Such striving may seem admirable, but it is the way of foolishness. Help them instead to find the wonder and the marvel of an ordinary life. Show them the joy of tasting tomatoes, apples and pears. Show them how to cry when pets and people die. Show them the infinite pleasure in the touch of a hand. And make the ordinary come alive for them. The extraordinary will take care of itself." — William Martin

"The secret of success is learning how to use pain and pleasure instead of having pain and pleasure use you. If you do that, you're in control of your life. If you don't, life controls you." – Tony Robbins

"Pleasure is, and must remain, a side effect or by-product, and is destroyed and spoiled to the degree to which it is a goal in itself." – Viktor Frankl

"I sometimes wonder if all pleasures are not substitutes for joy." – C.S. Lewis

"When a person can't find a deep sense of meaning, they distract themselves with pleasure." – Viktor Frankl

"The test and the use of man's education is that he finds pleasure in the exercise of his mind." – Jacques Barzun

Chapter 12: Imagine Happiness

How can you decide the best way to pursue happiness? It may begin with your imagination.

Kids in my neighborhood used to be fond of a game called "Would you rather...?" The kids would think up a pair of horrible options and ask questions like, "Would you rather poke your eye out with a spoon or scrape your tongue off with a cheese grater?"

I usually asked them a different type of question, something they didn't expect, like, "Would you rather be rich or stupid?"

The kids would pause to think it over, sampling both options in their imagination, wondering what the catch was, but there was no catch.

"Rich, of course!" they would finally shout.

"Good!" I would respond. "Because apparently you're not stupid."

One of the most useful things you can do with your amazing brain is to generate an idea in your imagination and taste it almost as if it were real.

This ability - if you use it - allows you to consider various plans, estimate their outcomes, then choose whichever path you deem most favorable.

A foolish person doesn't want to know the answer. They want to get drunk, drive home, and not think about the possibility of waking up in the hospital, or not waking up at all, in the morgue.

A wise person glances forward and allows their imagination to help steer their best path. They may not always get it exactly right, but they learn from their mistakes and make better choices the next time around.

WORKSHOP

Ponder & Discuss

1. How often do repeat whatever you usually do, as if on autopilot, without considering the consequences?
2. How often do you consider new actions or perspectives to try out, and wonder how they might turn out?
3. Who do you know who sometimes convinces you to try something new? How easily are you persuaded? How much do you resist?

Take Action

1. Think of something new to try that would make you happy - or something you haven't done for a long time, and give it a go. Ideally, bring someone else with you to share the ride. Afterward, discuss how it affected your happiness level.

In Other Words

"If I were to wish for anything, I should not wish for wealth and power, but for the passionate sense of what might be, for the eye which, ever young and ardent, sees the possible. Pleasure disappoints, possibility never. And what wine is so sparkling, what so fragrant, what so intoxicating as possibility." – Soren Kierkegaard

"You never change things by fighting the existing reality. To change something, build a new model that makes the existing model obsolete." – R. Buckminster Fuller

"You won't understand until you understand. Until then, keep your mind open to new possibilities." – Shaun Roundy

"Everyone has inside of her a piece of good news. The good news is that you don't know how great you can be. How much you can love. What you can accomplish. And what your potential is." – Anne Frank

"A mind once stretched by a new idea, never regains its original dimensions." – Oliver Wendell Holmes

Chapter 13: Relief

Heavy rain fell all night long at our Shadow Lake campsite, and now I sat on a large boulder while waiting for our tents to dry so we could pack them up and continue our journey through Wyoming's Wind River Mountains.

While staring upward and watching heavy, low clouds scrape across the massive granite spires that formed the back side of the Cirque of the Towers, a movement to my left caught my attention.

An animal was hopping from rock to rock as I had seen squirrels do earlier, but I swiveled my head toward it to look anyway. It was much larger than a squirrel, and I next thought of a fox (which we had seen the day before) as my eyes turned and focused.

What I saw was a cat with such a pronounced black and white stripe running half way along its flank that I wondered, "What is *that?!*" as my mind searched its database for a striped cat that lives in the Rockies.

Finally, the long, thin tail unmistakably identified the animal as a mountain lion.

It stopped in its tracks twenty feet away the moment it noticed me perched atop the boulder, and we stared into each others' eyes for a full twenty seconds before it turned and bounded away, pausing after a hundred feet to turn back and glance at me over its shoulder once more.

Our four-day, 24-mile trip provided some of the most stunningly gorgeous scenery of my life, but when I arrived at camp the second night, I hardly cared. We had only hiked eleven miles with 2,400 feet of elevation gain that day, but I had packed too heavily and felt exhausted.

Jenny tried to make conversation as we drew near the lake, but I only gave short answers and put all my energy into dragging one foot in front of the other as we wandered around and searched for a level campsite. All I wanted was to drop my pack and rest.

Sometimes the best source of happiness is simply relief. It's simply setting down your heavy load for a while and taking a breather.

Mental and emotional loads can weigh you down even more than physical ones, and they're usually harder to set aside for a rest.

Sometimes the loads aren't even terribly heavy, but you've carried them long enough to sap your strength and steal all the joy and beauty from living.

Whatever your personal load may consist of, there's always at least a partial solution available. You may choose to change your circumstances in small or significant ways, or simply change your perspective or attitude to something more self-supporting. Maybe an extra ounce of courage will you pull you through to the other side.

You should certainly consider seeking support from people who care about you, or from professionals trained to tackle your specific type of challenge.

Even a brief respite can make a world of difference.

With our tents mostly dried out, we packed up, and I followed Jenny and the others up the trail, now feeling rejuvenated and able to enjoy the stunning views along the way.

Climbing 1,200 steep feet over Texas Pass required a slow, methodical, continuous effort, but we made it, and the windy snowstorm that met us there did not daunt us.

For the rest of the afternoon, we watched cloud shadows roil against Pingora and Wolf's Back, felt sharp thunder rattle our bones as we lay in the grass near Lonesome Lake, then climbed back up another thousand feet to Jackass Pass on our way to Arrowhead Lake and our final campsite of the trip.

On day four, it felt good to get back to the parking lot and drop my pack in the truck bed. Not only because the demanding ordeal was over, but because we had experienced it all, and that felt satisfying and memorable.

All journeys end, sooner or later, one way or another. Enjoy the journey better by lightening your load and taking breaks as needed.

Ponder & Discuss
1. What heavy loads do you carry? How long have you endured them?
2. In what ways do they wear you down and reduce your happiness?
3. How can you set them aside for a while? Or maybe forever? Where could you find support to make them feel lighter?

Take Action
1. Take a break or get support for at least one of the loads you carry. If you believe you can't take a break right now, then at least imagine taking a break, and brainstorm ways you could get a breather.

P.S. Watch our fun trip video of Shadow Lake and the Cirque of the Towers at bit.ly/cirquetowers

In Other Words

"I am strong, but I am tired." - Unknown

"Oh, the comfort, the inexpressible comfort of feeling safe with a person; having neither to weigh thoughts nor measure word, but to pour them all out, just as they are, chaff and grain together, knowing that a faithful hand will take and sift them, keep what is worth keeping, and then, with the breath of kindness, blow the rest away." – George Eliot

"Relax. Nothing is under control." – Unknown

Chapter 14: Laughter

Pastor Bob, a pious man, beloved by all who knew him, had presided over his congregation for 22 years. He had comforted those who mourned, loved those who many considered unlovable, and helped many to stay on (or return to) the strait and narrow path. The whole community knew him as simply the Pastor.

When a long-time parishioner moved away, he invited her to address the congregation and say her good-byes to everyone at once.

It came out almost like a eulogy. She eloquently thanked longtime friends for kindnesses remembered, laughed at some humorous misunderstandings they endured, and, inevitably, when it came time to bid everyone farewell and state that she didn't know if they would ever meet again, there wasn't a single dry eye in the room, and she broke down in tears.

When her sobbing continued for nearly a minute and the congregation began to grow uncomfortable, Bob stood up next to the woman and put a comforting arm around her shoulders.

"I'm sorry, Pastor," the woman said in an unsteady voice, "for being such a big boob."

"That's alright," Bob replied. "The Pastor loves big boobs."

Bob's face had turned bright red before the first snicker began, but that immediately erupted into a roar of laughter from every soul in the room.

The surprise of the unintended double entendre, along with the juxtaposition of such a pure soul saying such a bawdy phrase was too much to keep inside, and renewed streams of tears now flowed freely down everyone's cheeks.

They politely tried to suppress their laughter when they noticed the Pastor's discomfort, but somehow that only made them laugh even harder, and for the remainder of the service, even in the middle of a hymn or prayer, someone would snicker and the room would burst into renewed, raucous, unconstrainable laughter.

After several weeks had passed and Pastor Bob recovered from his embarrassment, everyone recognized the event as the most joyous goodbye they had ever experienced, and if they could do it all over again, they agreed that they wouldn't change a thing.

Laughter is healing, which is one reason we joke about shocking tragedies, even when it elicits responses of "Too soon!"

We laugh in elation and frustration and discovery and joy. We admire the hero who laughs in the face of danger, and envy the successful businessperson who laughs all the way to the bank.

If laughter is so healthy, and if it contributes so much happiness and relief to our often-mundane lives, why not do it more often?

Why take life so seriously? Why not focus on the good all around, and the comical, and react less sensitively and critically, and imagine that everything is just fine, as if the winning Publisher's Clearinghouse sweepstakes number is already waiting for you in your mailbox? That's almost as likely as many of the things you worry about, and if it helps you laugh more readily and brightens your world and everyone's around you, then you win a different sort of sweepstakes with every chuckle.

Of course, there are different types of laughter, which sow different amounts of happiness. You may respond to irony or cruel cleverness with a sardonic laugh, but that can not lift your spirits as high as true mirth, if at all.

The next chapter explores those nuances while explaining how humor happens, but for now, at least decide to learn to laugh more often and freely and reap its many happiness-enhancing benefits.

Ponder & Discuss

1. How often do you laugh? What sort of thing do you typically laugh at? How does it make you feel?
2. List your friends or acquaintances who seem to laugh most often and most enjoyably. What's their secret? How do they make that happen? Would you like to laugh as often as them? How could you become more like them?

Take Action

1. Choose something that will make you laugh and do it. Watch a funny movie. Get together with friends and share humorous stories. When things go wrong, laugh it off and continue moving forward.

   Then write a few paragraphs about how it felt and how it influenced your mood and outlook on life, in order to increase your understanding and appreciation of laughter, which will motivate you to seek opportunities to laugh more often.

In Other Words

"The world is a looking-glass, and gives back to every man the reflection of his own face. Frown at it, and it in turn will look sourly at you; laugh at it, and with it, and it is a jolly, kind companion." – William Makespeace Thatckeray

"You can tell happiness by a smile or a laugh. But joy, real joy, is something else, something that only the eyes reveal. They seem to look out and in at the same time, loving both self and other, judging neither." – Mary Ylvisaker Nilsen

"He had an idea that even when beaten he could steal a little victory by laughing at defeat." – John Steinbeck

"He who laughs, lasts." – Mary Pettibone Poole

"I don't think existence wants you to be serious. I have not seen a serious tree. I have not seen a serious bird. I have not seen a serious sunrise. I have not seen a serious starry night. It seems they are all laughing in their own ways, dancing in their own ways. We may not understand it, but there is a subtle feeling that the whole existence is a celebration." – Osho

Chapter 15: Humor

"It is better to have loved and lost," my Grandmother wisely quipped during dinner one night, "than to buy shoes for eight children."

That was the funniest thing I ever heard her say. She died a few years later, and although she rarely told jokes, this single instance permanently paints my memory of her, adding a lighter hue to my fading recollection of her personality.

Laughter can work the same way. Even if a joke or situation only elicits a fleeting chuckle, that moment can paint your mood for hours as it launches you in a more mirthful trajectory - especially if you allow it to.

Laugh even more, and your mood continues to rise, lifting you ever nearer to heaven.

But not all laughter is created equal, and it would serve you well to understand how humor works, so you can search for and find it more often and more effectively.

Put simply, humor happens due to sudden flurries of mental activity, which your brain finds so delightful that you laugh out loud.

Let's explore a few common ways to generate laughter and reap its rewards of increased happiness.

Surprise

The key to a good joke is to prepare all the pieces, so when you reach the punch line or suddenly combine the pieces in an unexpected way, it's effortless for listeners' brains to immediately rearrange them, and laughter ensues.

Observe your brain as it interprets these stories, for example:

> Yesterday I went swimming at the local pool, and took a pee in the deep end. The lifeguard noticed, and blew his whistle so freaking loud that I nearly fell in.

You probably began by imagining the common experience of secretly releasing the pressure of your bladder and creating a warm spot in the pool while you swim. The last four words of the story change that image completely. Ambiguity, which you didn't even notice initially, gets clarified in an unexpected way.

> Liquor store employee: Do you need help?
> Me: Yes, but I decided to come here instead.
>
> A child comes home from her first day at school. "Well?" her father asks, "What did you learn today?" "Not enough," his daughter replies. "They want me to go back tomorrow."

Many of my neighbors adore a popular comedian and quote him endlessly, cracking themselves up as they repeat his comical tales and wry observations.

Me? I don't find him funny. They win, I lose, because I usually anticipate his punch lines two or three seconds too soon, so they don't surprise me, and he doesn't make me laugh.

If you don't enjoy puns, then you can relate. You may have loved them in second grade, but now they simply don't surprise you enough for you to enjoy them. They don't generate much mental spin, so they don't make you laugh.

> Q: What do you call a fake noodle?
> A: An impasta.
>
> Q: Why did the blind man fall into the well?
> A: Because he couldn't see that well.
>
> Q: What did the fisherman say to the magician?
> A: Pick a cod, any cod.
>
> Q: Why don't monsters eat clowns?
> A: Because they taste funny.

Subconscious Violations

The subconscious mind needs things to make simple sense. It processes thought primarily through images, which don't handle the complex abstractions well which your conscious mind navigates so adroitly.

Various types of jokes violate its simplistic world view, and as it scrambles to reduce the information to comfortable simplicity, the neural activity can tickle your funny bone.

Here are three ways to make that happen:

1. Nonsense: if something doesn't make sense, the mind will never succeed at rectifying it, though it may try for long enough to make you laugh.

> Q: What's the difference between a duck?
> A: One has webbed feet, and the other one does.

2. Juxtaposition: placing things together which don't match, such as acting out of character (adults acting like children, children acting like adults, animals acting like people, etc.), creates a sense of dissonance, and the subconscious mind can't stand dissonance, so it races to resolve it.

> A whale walks into a bar and makes a typical low-pitched, undulating, whale sound.
> "Go home, Eddie," the bartender says, "You're drunk."

3. Taboo: Your brain doesn't like unsolved problems (which explains why mysteries and bad news capture our attention so readily). So if something is taboo, then it's inappropriate, it violates what's accepted, and the subconscious sees that as a "problem."

As your brain spins to find a solution (which it doesn't find, unless it can remove the taboo), it causes that same whirlwind of neural activity which makes 2nd graders laugh at fart jokes, but not adults, who no longer get in trouble for saying the word "fart," but may choose not to because dwelling on it makes them look childish.

> Today I got in touch with my inner self...and that's why I will never again buy single-ply toilet paper.

Joy

Sometimes laughter works backwards - the joy happens first, and laughter follows, echoing the happiness, confirming it, celebrating and sharing it.

Sarcasm

Sarcasm can make us laugh when it's clever, but it may fail to lift your mood as much as other types for two reasons.

In the first place, it can be mean-spirited and intended to make others look foolish. If you believe that putting others down elevates you, then you may enjoy the cruelty, but it's an ugly humor, only a distant cousin to joyful mirth, and certainly the black sheep of the humor family.

In the second place, it's often used to escape vulnerability, to play it safe by not expressing and exposing your true thoughts and feelings, and hiding behind sarcasm makes it impossible to enjoy the richer joys of connection and honest self-expression.

WORKSHOP

Ponder & Discuss

1. Which types of humor do you enjoy most? Why?
2. Do you actively seek to enjoy humor, or are you at least usually ready to laugh, or must funny walk up and kick you in the shins to get your attention because you're too tied up in worry and busy-ness and the seriousness of life?
3. If you could blow out your birthday candles and make a wish to find life funny more often, and if that wish would come true, would you? Or do you prefer to be serious? Why?

Take Action

1. Watch a funny movie or TV series that you enjoy. Observe how it feels to laugh, where you feel it physically in your body, how it affects your general outlook, and how long that effect lasts.
2. Next time you laugh, allow that feeling and perspective to endure, replacing other feelings and perspectives, for as long as possible.

In Other Words

"He who laughs, lasts." – Mary Pettibone Poole

"It is more fitting for a [wo]man to laugh at life than to lament over it." - Seneca

"Always laugh when you can; it is a cheap medicine. Merriment is a philosophy not well understood. It is the sunny side of existence." – Lord Byron

"To laugh often and much, to win the respect of intelligent people and affection of children; to earn the appreciation of honest critics and endure the betrayal of false friends; to appreciate beauty, to find the best in others; to leave the world a bit better, whether by a healthy child, a garden patch, or a redeemed soul; to know even one life has breathed easier because you have lived. That is to have succeeded." – Ralph Waldo Emerson

Chapter 16: Meaning

I was 13 years old and finishing up one of my final soccer league games of the season. The score was 8 to 1, and I had kicked 7 of our points into our opponents' net.

I misplaced my shin guards before the game and played without them, and now sported painful dents up and down my shins where I had been kicked while jockeying for the ball, along with a purple-polka-dot pattern of bruises on my left calf where an opponent's cleat had landed on me as I skidded to one knee and kicked with my other foot.

My skills had dramatically improved this season because I signed up late and got assigned to the worst team in the league. Besides me, we started with two other players coordinated enough to walk and chew bubble gum at the same time. One was the goalie and the other one quit after we lost the first two games.

That meant I not only got to play every minute of every game, but I played the entire field, working with other forwards to move the ball up the field toward the far goal, and running back to defend alongside the half-backs and full-backs when we failed.

Not many years earlier, I showed no propensity for team sports whatsoever. Dad and I never played catch and I barely knew how to swing a bat. Our preferred activities were skiing, camping, and riding motorcycles on dirt roads.

I was a shy, overly sensitive kid, and looking back, it surprises me to recall how much I ran up and down the field, how hard I tried, never giving up until the clock ran out.

Despite our best efforts, we lost every single game - until tonight. Tonight we scrimmaged the second-worst team in the league, who we would play officially at ten a.m. the next morning.

When you analyze sports quickly and rationally, you have to admit that most games are pointless, meaningless. Soccer consists of eleven people trying to kick a small object into a net. While they kick the object back and forth, eleven others try to stop them and kick the object into the other net.

But look again and you'll see that sports are designed to draw out the intensity of living far more effectively than nearly any other activity: effort, struggle, triumph and defeat. Guts, glory, and mastery. Courage and heart. Determination and resilience.

Look once more and you'll see dozens or millions of fans watching from the sidelines or television screens, screaming their guts out for their team, contributing nothing to the outcome, yet taking wins and losses as personally as if the sweat and scrapes were their own, as if they deserved a spot on the podium and the front page along with the players.

As it turns out, meaning is subjective. It's entirely up to you, and nobody gets to tell you where to find it. So find it wherever you want. Drink it in and let it make you feel alive, purposeful and happy.

Classic sources of meaning come from contributing to something larger than yourself and somehow making life better for others. But you can also find significance and satisfaction through goals and accomplishment, learning and mastery, fun and memorable experiences - especially when shared; or through conscious awareness, such as when experiencing beauty and awe.

You don't even need to contribute or accomplish anything new. Look back at whatever you've already done today, or this week, or twenty years ago - it hardly matters when - and recognize the value it added to your life or to the wider world around you. Bask in the sense of satisfaction that such observation generates.

During that last soccer season, I tried my best to win, and partially because that never happened, I found my greatest enjoyments in teamwork and individual plays - a good pass, a block or a steal, and the occasional goal.

It was the little things that made me happy, that I reflected on after a game, that I clung to to keep me motivated, to keep me running up and down the field for the entire season.

Soccer offered me a whole new way to be, a trap door to escape the shy kid I had grown up as and become something more without ever realizing what was happening to me.

When the scrimmage ended, my teammates gathered together to celebrate our first victory, and the coach from the other team strode across the field toward us.

When he arrived, he held out his beefy hand toward me, and I vividly recall the image of his fluffy, red beard and wide, blue eyes as he said something like, "You're an amazing soccer player!" I shook his hand and drank in the praise, the long-awaited recompense for all my efforts, the recognition that I had skills, that I was *good*.

The next morning, we faced each other once more on a field at the nearby university and my team lost. My teammates played lazily, hardly trying, it seemed to me, and we only scored one goal to their three.

That made it official. We were the worst team in the league with no Disney-style underdog comeback ending to redeem us. The clock had run out for the last time.

I should have signed up to play again the next year. With my improved skills, I might have enjoyed some game time on a better team. I shouldn't have lost heart and given up, but I did. I skipped soccer camp the next summer and never played league ball again.

To some, the most meaningful part of sports is the score. You either win or lose, and nothing else matters. Second place only makes you the first loser.

To others, it's how you play the game, how much you enjoy the challenge, how it makes you grow and become - hopefully - a better human being as a result.

This time, I let the wrong meaning matter, and in the final tally, not continuing to play was the only loss that counts.

Ponder & Discuss

1. Now it's your turn. What feels meaningful in your life? What do you do that matters? What do you care deeply about? List five things you've done in the past which you continue to find meaningful and satisfying.
2. List your top five current most meaningful activities, relationships, possessions, or whatever else brings you happiness through a sense of significance.
3. What important things do you do regularly which don't feel very meaningful? Are they truly not, or do you merely fail to see that they are?
4. Discuss one or two of these with friends or strangers, and find out one or two things that they find meaningful in their lives.

   How much happiness do these things generate, and what flavor of happiness do they supply? Are they joyful and do they make you want to celebrate? Are they purposeful and satisfying? Do they drive you and help you focus on the flow of the present moment? Do they connect you with like-minded people or move you nearer to a better future?

Take Action

1. Do something about one of your list items and observe how it makes you feel, both immediately and days later. Write down your reaction or discuss it with others.
2. Find meaning in your least-favorite obligations. Why do they matter? How do they make the world a better place for you or others? How could you make them matter even more? Write a paragraph about how finding meaning makes unpleasant tasks more appealing, or less detestable.

In Other Words

"Life is not primarily a quest for pleasure, as Freud believed, or a quest for power, as Alfred Adler taught, but a quest for meaning. The greatest task for any person is to find meaning in his or her own life." – Viktor Frankl

"The Bushmen in the Kalahari Desert talk about the two 'hungers.' There is the Great Hunger and there is the Little Hunger. The Little Hunger wants food for the belly; but the Great Hunger, the greatest hunger of all, is the hunger for meaning… There is ultimately only one thing that makes human beings deeply and profoundly bitter, and that is to have thrust upon them a life without meaning. There is nothing wrong in searching for happiness. But of far more comfort to the soul is something greater than happiness or unhappiness, and that is meaning. Because meaning transfigures all. Once what you are doing has for you meaning, it is irrelevant whether you're happy or unhappy. You are content – you are not alone in your Spirit – you belong." – Laurens van der Post

"We don't seek the painful experiences that hew our identities, but we seek our identities in the wake of painful experiences. We can not bear a pointless torment, but we can endure great pain if we believe that it's purposeful." – Andrew Solomon

"Life is never made unbearable by circumstances, but only by lack of meaning and purpose." – Viktor Frankl

"The greatest task for any person is to find meaning in his or her life." – Viktor Frankl

Chapter 17: Good Company

"Let's walk down the beach," I suggested, but Teri had other ideas.

Two days earlier, my girlfriend Cindy and her two roommates climbed into my Celica and I steered it toward Los Angeles. One of them had a sister in Santa Monica where we could stay, which left us free to fill spring break with whatever adventures we chose to enjoy.

I wanted to walk down the beach. The night was dark, and glossy black ribbons would appear from the matte-black ocean, shimmer momentarily in the near-perfect darkness, then suddenly topple and rush up the steep beach toward us, each time creating the illusion that the wave was about to crash over our heads and perhaps wash us out to sea, though in reality only the tiniest bit of surf ever reached the top of the embankment where we stood. I found it beautiful and thrilling and memorable and a worthwhile way to get to the pier where we planned to buy some ice cream and enjoy the warm, offshore breeze.

Teri wanted to walk down the street where boys were driving by, looking for girls to pick up. I'm not sure what she'd have done if one of the boys had stopped, and other than Cindy, I didn't think the girls were terribly attractive, not the type that most boys would want to pick up, so I hardly saw the point.

Teri wasn't wrong to want to smile at the boys, and neither was I for wanting to stroll along the ocean, we simply had different ideas of what would be most fun. We all wanted the same thing - to do whatever would generate the most happiness - but we had different ideas about how to achieve that goal.

In the end, we compromised, walking the sand on the way to the pier, and the sidewalk on the way back, and I made a mental note to choose my adventure partners more carefully, to travel with people who more closely shared my interests and priorities.

Ponder & Discuss
1. List a few people who you enjoy being around. What do you like about their company?
2. How comfortable are you with openness and vulnerability?

Or do you hide behind shallow, impersonal topics or sarcasm? How do you think this affects your happiness level?
3. Describe an event where you did not enjoy the people around you. Why not? What would have improved the experience?
4. Was Terry's plan to gain some happiness as valid as mine? Why or why not?

Take Action

1. Schedule some time with one of your favorite people - invite or just call. Let yourself be genuine, open, and vulnerable. Then discuss or write a paragraph about how that affected your happiness - both in the moment and days later.

In Other Words

"Which is more important," asked Big Panda, "the journey or the destination?"
"The company," said Tiny Dragon. – James Norbury

"You're always with yourself, so you might as well enjoy the company." – Diane Von Furstenberg

"Next time you feel the urge to change someone, love them instead. Love changes people." – Unknown

"If you look at the people in your circle and don't get inspired, then you don't have a circle, you have a cage." – Nipsey Hussle

"If you want to be a leader who attracts quality people, the key is to become a person of quality yourself." – Jim Rohn

"People who shine from within don't need the spotlight." – Unknown

Chapter 18: Think Happy Thoughts

All summer long, Kirsten and other college neighbors would come with me to the dam. We'd bring our homework, lay blankets on the sand, and read until someone got tired of studying and shouted, "Last one in's a rotten egg!"

Then we all flipped our textbooks upside down to save our place, jumped to our feet, ran down the beach, and dove in to the lake. It was our only rule. We could not refuse.

One detail I recall when I think of Kirsten was a sticker on her notebook that said "Think happy thoughts" along with a cheery yellow smiley face. It seemed like a motto she took to heart, and I loved her for the way her happy smile and upbeat attitude always brightened my day.

As autumn arrived and temperatures cooled, our dam study sessions became infrequent, and only Kirsten and I went for the last one. We pulled the blanket over our shoulders, and I held my book loosely in my hands but stared out at the water while bittersweet nostalgia coursed through my veins.

I missed the idyllic summer days which seemed endless and mighty while the sun burned hot high in the sky, and so short and fragile now that its warmth had faded. I missed all the good memories and wished I could somehow bring them back to stay.

An idea crept into my mind, and with it, the corners of my mouth turned up slightly. "Last one in's..." I began to say when Kirsten cut me off abruptly.

"Don't you dare!" she said sharply, and by the serious yet lively and playful look in her eyes, I believed that if I finished the sentence, she would jump to her feet and run into the water with me, the last two lemmings plunging to our fate in the sea.

I paused and let the sentence die on my lips, smiled wistfully at her, then let the smile fade as I turned back to look over the water shimmering in the cool afternoon sun. "I miss summer," I confessed.

Half a minute passed before she replied. "Today's not so bad, either," she said, and then, in a blink, it *wasn't* so bad!

It was kind of good, in fact, kind of marvelous and satisfying, with a different type of warmth that smoldered inside rather than burning outwardly, and I felt happy all over again.

"Think happy thoughts."

I haven't seen Kirsten for decades now, yet the phrase still haunts my memory.

"Think happy thoughts." Such simple advice, yet so infinitely wise and effective.

As the intervening years have slid by, the summers and autumns and winters and springs as the sun rose and fell across the sky, I wish I had remembered and applied her notebook's counsel more faithfully. If I had, I know things would have turned out even better.

Don't let another precious day go to waste. Consciously, doggedly, intentionally, cheerfully, gratefully, humbly, enthusiastically, undyingly Think. Happy. Thoughts.

When you do, you'll discover as I did, that today is kind of marvelous after all.

Ponder & Discuss

1. What are "happy thoughts"? How much do they affect your happiness? Why?
2. Write down at least three happy thoughts you can use over and over. Here are a few example happy thoughts to get you started:
   A. Today is kind of marvelous.
   B. I'm a grown up, which means I can buy a donut WHENEVER I WANT!
   C. I am strong and happy and fortunate.
   D. Wherever I look for good, I find some.

Take Action

1. Say or think each of your happy thoughts at least ten or twenty times per day until they become habit.
2. As soon as you notice them making a difference, share your experience with someone else.

In Other Words

"Those who enjoy happiness do so because they have earned it with their thoughts." – Alan Cohen

"When one door of happiness closes, another opens, but often we look so long at the closed door that we do not see the one that has been opened for us." –Helen Keller

"The most welcomed people of the world are never those who continually look back upon the trials, the sorrows, the failures, the bitter frustrations of yesterday, but those who cast their eyes forward with faith, hope… courage, happy curiosity." – James Francis Cooke

"Every man has a train of thought on which he rides when he is alone. The dignity and nobility of his life, as well as his happiness, depend upon the direction in which that train is going, the baggage it carries, and the scenery through which it travels." – John Fort Newton

"Happiness is not something to be found somewhere, it is a state of mind." – Charles Steves

Chapter 19: Inches

There's a deep cave across the lake from my home with a tube-like passage through solid rock that's so narrow that I can't fit through unless I extend one arm out in front of me.

I nudge my way forward an inch at a time with toes and finger tips for over a hundred feet until the passageway makes a sharp right turn and opens into a small room large enough to turn around and head back the way I came.

Sometimes I would crawl through with friends. We'd drive to the West Desert before sunset, slide through the narrow cave entrance on our stomach, and not emerge again until the Milky Way had spun half way across the night sky. Then we would lie on our backs and watch for falling stars while owls glided silently overhead, searching for an unsuspecting dinner of mice and rabbits.

Other times I would go with my search and rescue team when cavers got trapped in the cave's maze-like depths.

These emergencies usually weren't too serious. We would find the cavers wedged in narrow, awkward passages where perhaps they shouldn't have tried to fit in the first place, but we trusted in our ability to get them out.

The cavers didn't always feel as calm. They wanted to escape their stone prison and regain their freedom by yards, by leaps and bounds. They longed for the ability to take a full breath without their rib cage pressing against the constricting rock, or to move their legs and hips which somehow fit while crawling forward, but wouldn't allow them to reverse their direction.

We would bring bright lights and oxygen, and tell jokes to keep them calm, then patiently lift, twist, push and pull, satisfied to make an inch of progress at a time, and soon enough, our patients would find themselves free once more, and hopefully wiser for the experience.

Happiness seekers often think and behave the same way as those stuck cavers. They find themselves wedged, trapped, unhappy and desperate, and seemingly unable to work themselves free. They wonder if they will ever again see the light of day or take in a deep, satisfying breath of fresh air on the surface.

It's hard to see the path back to happiness when the world around them looks so dark and unwielding.

"If only I had a better job!" they might reason. "If only I could catch a break, or fall in love, or win the lottery, or lose weight, or take that vacation, or get more likes on social media," or any other number of solutions to their sadness or discontent. Happiness looks like it's a million miles away and they understandably want to get there as quickly as possible!

But in most cases, happiness arrives by inches, not yards. It grows by trying new approaches and forming new habits, by changing thoughts and behaviors in ways that lift them up, or that prevent them from getting stuck in the first place.

Some of the happiness techniques you'll find in this book can generate immediate, notable, lasting improvements. Once you give them a try, you'll see yourself or the world from a new perspective, and you can never return to your old point of view.

But if you ever feel like you're only inching toward happiness, do not feel discouraged, because that's the way out. That's the way up. Keep inching toward happiness, and soon enough, you'll find yourself free.

WORKSHOP

Ponder & Discuss

1. List two or three things that would make you happy immediately.

2. List two or things that would make you happy slowly or incrementally.
3. Which of those things would contribute the most happiness over the next week, month, year, and decade?
4. If you could only choose one item from your lists, which would you take?

Take Action

1. Do something right now that will contribute to your happiness only after you've finished. Tidy up some corner of your home. Do a dozen sit-ups (or a hundred, if you find a dozen too easy). Then write a paragraph about how doing such things a dozen times a day might change your life for the better.

In Other Words

"What does it take to be happy? Progress. Progress equals happiness. Even if you're not where you want to be yet, if you are on the road, if you're improving, if you are making progress, you're going to love it. You're going to feel alive." – Tony Robbins

"You must learn to walk to the edge of the light, then a few steps into the darkness, then the light will appear." – Spencer Kimball

"When you dance, your purpose is not to get to a certain place on the floor. It's to enjoy each step along the way." – Wayne Dyer

Chapter 20: Enjoy Yourself

In high school, my brothers and I drove an old yellow Toyota Corolla hatchback we named The Piece; as in, the piece of crap. Despite the derogatory name, and despite the fact that we didn't treat it very well, we loved that car for all the experiences it made possible.

We drove it to the dam on hot summer days to jump off the cliffs and cool down. We sped up dirt roads in local canyons, learning to swerve to avoid rocks when the car lacked the clearance to drive over them.

We never felt ashamed by the rusted-out floorboard in the back seat, which we covered with a thin sheet of steel which we could lift and drop smoke bombs through just as the light turned green and we drove away, leaving a cloud of green smoke for cars behind us to drive through and wonder about.

We weren't embarrassed that it wasn't as nice as other cars, and because we were always having fun, nobody else seemed to mind riding in it, either. One afternoon, we crowded 13 kids inside and drove them home after school. The little engine barely got us up the hill to our neighborhood, but everybody preferred the good company and cramped quarters to riding the bus.

But this chapter isn't really about our old car, it's about you. It's about the times you don't feel good enough, and the times you don't stand tall because you're not as polished as other people. It's about the times you feel like crap and decide to stay home rather than dive into life and whatever grand adventures it offers.

No matter how unimpressive you may look or feel, how weak your engine, or how old and rusty your frame; your body, heart, mind and soul make up the only vehicle you've got to carry you through the rest of your life, and it's up to you to make the most of it and enjoy the ride.

If you catch yourself thinking, "If only I was smarter/ funnier/ richer/ cooler/ sexier...*then* I'd be happy!" then you're doing it wrong. You're doing it backwards, or inside out.

Such thoughts mean you have externalized your source of happiness, assigned it to inanimate objects, or to other people or experiences, and made mood and self-image depend on what *they* think of you, how *they* react to you, and that makes happiness inherently insecure and unfulfilling.

Even if you've bought in to the "contest" of life and happen to be winning, even if you're the current King of Bunker Hill, you'll always have to fight to defend your perch, and sooner or later, someone will knock you from your place at the top. What will you do to be happy then?

That's simply not the way happiness is designed to work.

Want proof? Look around and you'll find plenty of smart, funny, wealthy, cool, sexy, *unhappy* people. You may look at them and think, "They have *no right* to be unhappy! If I could trade places with them, I would be ecstatic! I would be loved and appreciated and feel ridiculously happy every single day!"

But in reality, you wouldn't. Those people need to learn to be happy from the inside out the same as you.

Besides, it's not fair to make anyone else responsible for your happiness. If you think you'd be happy if someone would love and accept you just as you are; or respect your opinion and agree with everything you say, or if they treated you the way you want to be treated, then once again, you're doing it wrong.

All those things might be nice, but when you finally get it right, when you internalize your main source of happiness, when you generate your happiness independently of whatever circumstances you find yourself in, or what anybody else thinks of you, then you'll scarcely need them anymore. You'll be totally, absolutely, one-hundred percent fine no matter what they say or do.

True, lasting, secure happiness and being okay has to come from within yourself, and nowhere else. Perhaps we need to start using the term "self-happiness," sort of like "self-esteem" and "self-love," because no one else can take your place. Nobody can do it for you.

Even if our car wasn't the prettiest, fastest, or most expensive, we loved it anyway, and that made us winners amongst our friends.

That's how you should feel about yourself, too. We loved it because we made good use of it and shared wonderful experiences, and that's what you ought to do with yourself, too.

We rejected consumerism, without realizing what we were doing We paid no attention to marketer's messages that happiness only comes from having the best of everything, that only beautiful things deserve to be loved and appreciated, and we enjoyed ourselves and our lives as richly as we could have done with a hundred times more money in the bank.

Ponder & Discuss

1. List three situations where you feel not good enough to belong, or where you don't feel comfortable enough to fully express yourself, and explain why not?
2. What would happen if you stood up tall and showed up in your full glory anyway? Would others accept you as the person you present to the world? Or would they laugh and mock you for trying?
3. If they wouldn't accept you and let you live your best life, are those the kind of people whose opinions you should care about in the first place? How can you learn to pay them no heed?

Take Action

1. Leave your phone at home and take a walk alone somewhere pleasant. In this moment, is your happiness hobbled by not having more possessions? Or by being alone and having no one to love you or stroke your ego? Why not be that happiness-independent all the time?

In Other Words

"Taking care of myself doesn't mean 'me first.' It means 'me, too.'" – L.R. Knost

"One of the best ways to learn to judge yourself more kindly is to practice on others." – Shaun Roundy

"What is necessary to change a person is to change his awareness of himself." – Abraham Maslow

"The way you talk to yourself about yourself both reveals and creates who you think you are, which determines your life experience." – Shaun Roundy

"You change the world by being yourself." – Yoko Ono

Chapter 21: Delusions of Grandeur

Sometimes you invest in things and experiences you hope to reap happiness from, but they don't work as well as expected.

Such was the case when I dragged my feet across the 13,770-foot-high summit block of the Grand Teton, plopped down on a boulder, shed my pack, lay back against black granite, and sighed. Finally, the climb was over, and I felt relieved.

Yesterday we lugged our heavy gear six miles and 4,000 feet up the rocky path from where we left the car at the Lupine Meadows trailhead. This morning we crawled from our tents before dawn, choked down a tasteless breakfast, and climbed the first pitches of the full Exum Ridge in the dark with fingers numb from the cold.

While planning the expedition, I dreamt of taking a long fall from one of the cliffs I just climbed. I dreamt of the unforgettable thrill of looking hundreds of feet down as I whistled through the open sky, almost comfortable with the knowledge that whatever cam or hex or stopper I had wedged into the mountain and clipped to my rope would catch me safely.

I could then replay that memory for the rest of my life, smiling at the recollection of my doubled heart rate and the adrenaline-induced sense of being 100% present and awake and alive.

In reality, I had not placed a single piece of gear in several thousand feet of climbing that I felt comfortable falling on - that I could trust, without a doubt, to arrest my fall.

On the steepest pitches, placements were few and far between, sometimes 15 or 20 feet apart, where I wedged small steel cubes into shallow cracks as protection. If I slipped from 15 feet above one of those, I would drop for 30 feet before the rope began to catch me. If the piece blew its placement, I would fall another 30 or 40 feet, or hit the deck, whichever came first. No thank you!

While planning this expedition, dreaming of the glory of summitting one of the world's most beautiful and famous alpine ascents, I sometimes lamented that it wasn't 35 feet taller. That would make it the tallest mountain in Wyoming, raising it one foot above the remote Gannett Peak.

But now, feeling the drain of climbing in the thin atmosphere and with a splitting headache due to dehydration (the cold wind kept me from feeling thirsty, even though my body desperately needed water), I muttered to myself, "This is high enough."

I didn't complain, though. For one thing, that would do no good. For another, I didn't want to earn the nickname of the mountain itself - the Grand Teton, named by lonely French trappers which, in English, translates to "the Big Boob."

Gazing down to the east, I saw Disappointment Peak resting thousands of feet below us. Four climbers named that pinnacle in 1925 when they tried to summit the Grand from the shortest path possible, by climbing straight up the east ridge from Lupine Meadows, but they were stopped by an impassible 450' cliff separating the two peaks.

The obvious lesson from that lesser summit's name is to never lean your ladder against the wrong wall. Don't try to win happiness along routes that can't lead you there.

We all do that, of course, so we all have our own personal disappointment peaks.

We invest in relationships that don't last - not that we could have necessarily known better before giving them a try.

We avoid avoidable conflict that could have resolved or reduced our anxieties.

We procrastinate necessary but unpleasant tasks.

We agree to quick, shallow, fleeting fixes, then pay outrageous happiness costs for our unwise actions.

We ignore efforts and investments in ourselves and our lives that would have led us to glorious summits, simply because they sound like too much effort.

We do all this because we believe - or we do our best to convince ourselves - that we'll be happier this way, at least for the moment, and we try not to think about the future consequences that our actions - or inactions - inevitably bring.

Now take a minute to reflect, be honest with yourself - what are *your* disappointment peaks?

When do you pretend to deceive yourself and live smaller than you could, or should?

Which goals could you achieve if you simply tried - yet again and again you fail to put forth the effort?

How often do you lean your ladder against the wrong wall, and end up less happy as a result?

This books presents many valid sources of happiness, proven routes to lead you to the top, to make you king of your own mountain. I do my best to make them sound appealing and easy - which they often are! - but you must still invest your time, energy, and sometimes courage to turn them into realities in *your* life.

Great thinkers from Plato to Mills to Victor Frankl understood that you can't march *straight* to happiness. It doesn't work that way, and if you expect happiness to simply *happen* for no particular reason, then, once again, you're bound for disappointment.

In reality, happiness is the result of doing and being and thinking something else. So be grateful, be engaged, be expressive, connected, confident, curious, active, awake, inspired, alive, interested, hopeful, loving, forgiving, and take another step toward a worthwhile goal.

By the time we started down the easy way off the mountain, I had hydrated, rested a little, and I found myself feeling much better.

We climbed another summit the next day, then spent one more night nestled among the moraine's massive boulders before carrying our camping and climbing gear back down to the car.

Only then, from the highway leading us back home, only when I glanced back up at the mountain towering 7,000 feet over our heads as we drove away, as I breathed in the thick, oxygen-rich air at the lower elevation and noticed that I could say a long sentence or take a drink of water without needing to stop and catch my breath, only then did the full appreciation of our accomplishment strike me, and only then did the elation I expected to experience on the summit stretch my face into a wide, happy, satisfied grin.

I will never again look at the Grand Teton without remembering the feel of cold, rough granite against my fingertips, the breath of the cool breeze tousling my hair, and the glorious view from the summit, with the whole world falling dramatically away below my feet, with the jagged peaks of the other Tetons towering far below us.

Sometimes happiness requires suffering, and sometimes you must pre-pay for your enjoyable emotions. Sometimes the suffering is worth it. Sometimes the grandest, most glorious moments of your existence are also the worst, the hardest, and the most challenging.

Sometimes the easiest, most pleasant and appealing path is not the one you ought to travel. Don't be afraid to put in the effort required to live a happy life, and don't stroll blindly through life, always reacting, always taking the path of least resistance, only to eventually grow unhappy and wonder where everything went wrong.

WORKSHOP

Ponder & Discuss + Take Action

1. Write down five actions that would increase your happiness but that you avoid, or actions which undermine your happiness, but you do them anyway.
2. Pay attention each time you take a step up disappointment peak. Just notice, that's all. You don't have to change your

direction...unless you choose to.
3. Discuss this with others or journal about it now and then to deepen your awareness. Do not criticize yourself about it, that won't help. Just let your increased awareness work on you and do its magic, and your behaviors and motivations will naturally follow.

In Other Words

"Don't aim at success. The more you aim at it and make it a target, the more you are going to miss it. For success, like happiness, cannot be pursued; it must ensue, and it only does so as the unintended side effect of one's personal dedication to a cause greater than oneself or as the by-product of one's surrender to a person other than oneself. Happiness must happen, and the same holds for success: you have to let it happen by not caring about it." – Victor Frankl

"The more you make a relationship about what you're getting, the weaker the relationship is. An intimate relationship is not a place you go to get things; if you do that, you're always going to be disappointed. It's a place you go to give. If you can fall in love with someone so much that you live to light them up, and lighting them up lights you up, done deal." – Tony Robbins

"Twenty years from now you will be more disappointed by the things that you didn't do than by the ones you did do, so throw off the bowlines, sail away from safe harbor, catch the trade winds in your sails. Explore, Dream, Discover." –Mark Twain

Chapter 22: Nature is Nurture

As the sun rose all pink and fiery over the Atlantic Ocean, my rental car sat stranded in deep sand on a secluded beach somewhere along North Carolina's Outer Banks.

I watched the glorious red orb rise above the horizon for a while longer, sometimes closing my eyes to feel its warmth splash gently across my face from 93 million miles away, then turned away and got back to work.

By placing the car's floor mats on the soft sand, then setting the jack atop it, I was able to lift the car, one wheel at a time, high enough to lay six-feet-long 4x4" wooden posts under them.

Once in place, I climbed into the drivers seat, shifted into reverse, hit the gas, and drove about twenty feet farther from the ocean and nearer to the road before sinking in and becoming hopelessly stuck again. I would then open the door, climb out, and repeat the process.

I smiled at the fact that, attached to the 4x4 posts, were signs that read "No driving on beach beyond this point." I had uprooted them from where they stood in the sand to rescue myself from my little predicament.

I had been working at a newspaper near Virginia Beach, went to the airport to fly home for the weekend, dropped off the rental car, and checked the ticket for my flight's gate assignment. Only then did I realize that my tickets were not scheduled for today, but for *next* Friday. My travel coordinator had booked me over the weekend without me asking.

I went back and retrieved my rental car, glanced at the map and saw the nearby Outer Banks - a thin strand of sand reaching miles from the mainland, and said to myself, "That's it. That's where I'll spend the weekend."

Lucky for me, it was late March, early season, a bit too cold for most visitors, and I had the whole place nearly to myself. I checked in to rustic hotels along the beach, woke in time to watch the sun rise over the ocean, visited Kitty Hawk where Orville and Wilbur Wright flew the world's first airplane, toured lighthouses, sat on the beach and read, watched grasses bending over and etching circles around their stems as ocean winds shifted direction, followed dolphins with my eyes as they made their rounds up and down the coast, and imagined how it would feel to be a pelican, watching dozens of them diving endlessly into the ocean, moving seamlessly between atmospheres of bright, thin, cool air and dark, thick, cold water to scoop up their breakfast and fly away.

While riding ferries between islands, I fed the gulls, tossing bits of bread and cookies into the air, watching them dip or flare their wings to rise, fall, and deftly catch the meals in their beaks. The air pressure above and below their wings that carried them through the sky was invisible, at first, but soon I could sense it clearly, I felt it in my mind, I knew exactly how it felt to fly, and I thought out loud, "How could you live here and *not* invent the airplane?"

The weekend turned out extremely relaxing and refreshing, washing away all stress and restoring my connection with the natural world.

So as I repeatedly lifted my car from the sand where I had come to watch the sunrise and drove it off the beach twenty feet at a time, I didn't mind one bit that I had gotten stuck. It was well worth the trouble.

Thanks to modern research, the healing properties of spending time in nature are more than just anecdotal and common sense. Many scientific studies from around the world confirm the reduction in stress and contribution to peace and happiness that nature offers.

Call it vitamin N, and be sure to consume your recommended daily - or at least weekly, or monthly - dose.

Ponder & Discuss

1. What memories do you have of time spent outdoors, stepping on something other than tile, carpet or cement, and allowing it to calm and refresh you?
   How often do you do such things? When was the last you made time for nature?
2. Now compare your experience of the great outdoors to other environments where you spend most of your time and notice how they affect you differently.
   Are they more artificial, or noisy, or busy, or perhaps calm and pleasant? Do they add stress or maybe make you feel alive? Even if you love the concrete jungle, give nature a try and test

its proven benefits.
3. What natural areas are available to you nearby? Even if you don't have miles of sandy beaches or shady forests with solitary dirt paths, you could spend time in your back yard or try out a city park. You could turn off the AC in your car and roll down the windows, letting the wind run its invisible fingers through your hair.

Take Action
4. Don't only bloom where you are planted, plant yourself where you bloom, and make a commitment and plan to spend more time in nature. Afterward, observe and write a paragraph about how it affects your happiness.

In Other Words

"Keep close to Nature's heart… and break clear away, once in awhile, and climb a mountain or spend a week in the woods. Wash your spirit clean." – John Muir

"All truly great thoughts are conceived while walking." – Friedrich Nietzsche

"Ordinarily, I go to the woods alone, with not a single friend, for they are all smilers and talkers and therefore unsuitable. I don't really want to be witnessed talking to the catbirds or hugging the old black oak tree. I have my way of praying, as you no doubt have yours. Besides, when I am alone I can become invisible. I can sit on the top of a dune as motionless as an uprise of weeds, until the foxes run by unconcerned. I can hear the almost unhearable sound of the roses singing. If you have ever gone to the woods with me, I must love you very much." – Mary Oliver

Chapter 23: Play

When I look at photos from our arrival at Gunboat Island, about ten miles north of Panama's Caribbean coast, I'm struck by the dull, vacant deadness in the children's eyes.

Their parents paddled dugout canoes over to our 52-foot sailboat once we dropped anchor in the bay, and the children sat there quietly or climbed onto our boat's deck and stared listlessly forward, not taking a great deal of interest in anything.

David and I slept on the beach that night - our first night off the boat in weeks - where we occasionally woke to brush away the sand crabs crawling over our arms and faces.

The moon, falling ever nearer toward the horizon, sparkled on gentle waves as the tide crawled slowly up and down the beach, which lulled us back to sleep.

The warm sun woke us the next morning, and we greeted the children as they strolled by along the shore. Dan came ashore and gave them gifts of notebooks and pencils, along with some ointment for a festering sore we spotted on a baby the day before.

After breakfast, three children under ten years old joined us for a walk around the island, which would have taken about five minutes if we hadn't stopped to play.

One cute little girl took David's hand as we kicked lazily through the small waves washing up and down the beach, and I hoisted another to my shoulders for a ride, then pretended to nearly topple over one way, then the other, into the ocean. The children smiled happily at first, then laughed freely and gleefully.

Next, we picked up pieces of coral, drew a hopscotch course in the sand, and taught them how to toss the coral to each square in succession, hop along on one foot, bend over to pick up the coral and hop back.

They didn't speak much, and only hours later did I realize that only a few of the adults on the island spoke Spanish, while the kids didn't understand a single word I said.

The family showed us their home and explained how to build a thatched roof and how often it had to be replaced. We bought breadsticks for ten cents each and they taught us to shell coconuts on a sharp stick half buried in the ground, everyone laughing at my awkward first attempts.

By the time we left the island the next day, as we gave the kids a ride in the dingy powered by a speedy outboard motor and showed them around our luxurious 52' ketch, their eyes sparkled and danced. They laughed easily and often. They looked happy and awake, glowing with joy and life.

When I look back at the photographs of our departure, I'm struck by the contrast, by the difference that a few hours of play made in their countenances.

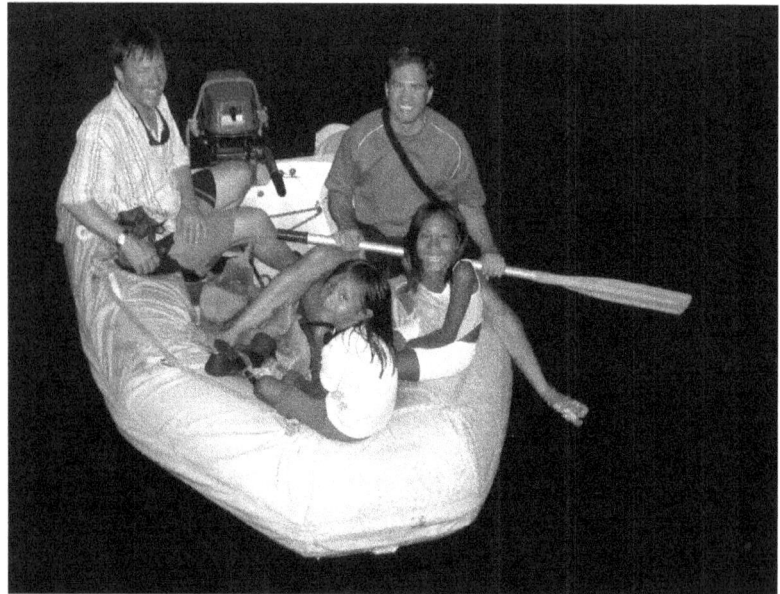

Some researchers blame the lack of play for our current epidemic of social anxiety and modern sociopolitical tensions. They say that only through self-directed play can children acquire the skills they need to navigate life's inevitable conflicts and frictions.

We're not robots, and if you treat yourself like one, you're bound to experience a few malfunctions. Your eyes may glaze over and you may slowly forget how to enjoy being alive.

How do you like to play? When was the last time you dropped all your cares and played with abandon? When was the last time your eyes lit up, and you found yourself fully immersed in the moment, content to be right here, right now, and nowhere else?

Or have you grown up, become responsible and serious, and learned to view play as an optional luxury, or even childish? When did you become a pirate, as Peter Pan would define you?

If you think you don't have time for play, then learn how to add more play to your schedule without taking up any additional time. Learn to combine play with your other activities.

While writing, when I get stuck on a particular concept or plot element, I go for a run to clear my mind. I wear a smartwatch and take notes along the way as the ideas grow clearer in my mind, and I end up doing some of my best writing on the dirt trails winding through the foothills above my home, so play makes work time *more* effective and I lose nothing.

If you can't get away from home or the office, you can imagine that you're in a play or movie, which adds interest to even life's most monotonous moments. In a movie, every word and action forms part of the plot. Every single detail matters. Look around and ask yourself: who are the main characters? Which one is a spy? Which ones are about to fall in love or get eaten by zombies? Which clues would an attentive audience member notice?

Of course this is all imaginary - probably...but that's the whole point! Let your imagination run wild for a change. It will do you good.

The more play you add to your life, the more balance and happiness it can contribute to your life, and the more clearly you will see that it's worth making a point to include play; that if you want to thrive, and not just survive, then letting play ignite the happy glow behind your eyes may be the surest path to take you there.

Ponder & Discuss

1. List at least three ways that you play (or could play, if you chose to).
2. Write or discuss what happiness and other value you get from those activities.
3. Do you find play more rewarding when you do it alone or with others? Why?

Take Action

1. Participate in one of your list items (or try something new!) and record the difference it makes in your mood both immediately and the following day or days later.

In Other Words

"The pinnacle of productivity is to never work; always play." – Marianne Williamson

"How many adventure films does it take to compensate for a lack of adventure? How many superhero movies must one watch, to compensate for the atrophied expression of one's greatness? How much pornography to meet the need for intimacy? How much entertainment to substitute for missing play?" – Charles Eisenstein

"Be enthusiastic till it thrills you. Display it, radiate it, till it infects all those around you." – Homi Kharas

"The opposite of play is not work – the opposite of play is depression." – Dr. Stuart Brown

"If you are depressed and anxious, you are not a machine with malfunctioning parts. You are a human being with unmet needs. The only real way out of our epidemic of despair is for all of us, together, to begin to meet those human needs – for deep connection, to the things that really matter in life." – Johann Hari

Chapter 24: Courage

Buying a kayak on Craigslist and paddling alone for 120 miles through Florida's Everglades sounded like a good idea when I planned it. What a grand, unforgettable adventure this would be!

But now, an hour after sunset on December 26, as I filled fresh water containers and loaded up the boat with ten days of supplies, I didn't want to go. I didn't want to paddle away into the dark mangrove forest with just the manatees, sharks, and crocodiles to keep me company.

But what else could I do? I was thousands of miles from home with no car, no hotel room, and no backup plan, so I shoved away from the dock in Naples and pointed the bow toward the Rookery Preserve and Ten Thousand Islands.

Every single day of the trip would prove daunting, paddling an average of thirteen miles per day, often into steady headwinds and miles from shore with waves washing over the side of the boat; sometimes getting lost in narrow, twisting, mangrove waterways, with crocodiles swimming alongside me, one of which snapped at me so loudly that it hurt my ears; plus all the solitude, which I sometimes found peaceful and other times lonely.

I had no choice but to continue on, and no one would even know if I got in trouble until I didn't show up in Flamingo next Wednesday evening when I had arranged to catch a ride to the airport with the park ranger who would also buy my kayak.

So I paddled into the darkness, checking my GPS now and then to help me steer through the inky darkness to my first campsite.

I woke in the morning and paddled twenty-one miles, scarcely pausing until I arrived at the next tiny island just after sunset, and repeated the pattern over and over for nine days, finding my hands unable to close more tightly than the circumference of the paddle each morning, and waking up the final morning to gale-force winds which snapped my tent in half, and which - luckily - I only had to paddle against once, and for less than a hundred yards, after taking a wrong turn, because paddling as furiously as I could only moved the boat forward inches at a time, and I could not afford to pause until I rounded the corner into the correct waterway.

For better or worse, life doesn't always require you to keep on paddling day in, day out. Too often it allows you to collapse, if you choose, to lie down and give up.

No one blames you when you decline invitations to live an adventurous life - instead they agree with you, that it's better to play it safe and avoid unnecessary risk.

But if you want to live happily ever after, and if you're not already doing so, then you more than likely must cross an ocean or two to get there, and you can't do that while lying on the couch watching reruns and filling your face with chips and soda.

Fear is mostly a survival mechanism, an impulse designed by the oldest part of your brain, evolutionarily speaking, to avoid risk and increase your chances of perpetuating the species.

This is the powerful part of your brain, the part that controls your emotions and twists all your perceptions to match its biases. It's the cause of 95% of your suffering. It's what keeps most people contained forever in their same old box, never progressing much, and never living out their fondest dreams.

That part of your brain doesn't care much for your happiness, so if you want to get it, you may have to let your conscious mind steer your course instead, which sometimes points you directly into the dark, frightening, disorienting, monster-filled forest of fear that your subconscious concocts to try to talk you out of it.

Lucky for you, your brain can be rewired. Facing your fears and watching everything turn out okay again and again retrains your brain to realize that some risks aren't so risky after all. Then it quits freaking out so much and allows you to live your best life in greater peace and enjoyment.

If you'd like to become more fearless (either through developing courage or eliminating fears one by one), then step one is to select a fear to face and overcome. Do you have something you've always wanted to do? Is there something you'd like to say, and someone you'd like to say it to? Even simply *imagining* doing or saying it seems so real to your subconscious that you can defuse your fears without taking a single physical step.

You can conquer fear an inch at a time or charge recklessly toward your fondest dreams, which invites your subconscious to send out its whole defensive army all at once, so you can try to defeat it in a single battle rather than risking death by a thousand strokes.

Take one step in that direction, and anxiety rises to the surface and screams its fool head off. "DON'T DO THAT!!!" it shouts - not because moving forward would be bad for you. It would certainly be better than staying stagnant where you are.

But because moving forward means change, and your subconscious detests change, and simply because it's unknown and therefore outside of your comfort zone, your subconscious does its best to stop you in your tracks and persuade you lie back down and give up.

Now for the good news: once you stretch your comfort zone and change your circumstances for the better, *that* becomes your new reality, and your subconscious will defend it just as adamantly as it resisted until you fought your way through fear, arrived at your new home, and settled in.

When I paddled away from the dock into the mangrove forest, I couldn't help but imagine crocodiles and sharks swimming nearby, invisible in the darkness and hidden by the opaque waters on which I floated, but I kept paddling anyway.

With every passing day, with every mile and island and ocean and river that fell behind me, my confidence grew that I had what it would take to reach my destination nine days later.

It was a great relief to finally drag my boat up the concrete ramp in Flamingo, but it also felt rewarding to have accomplished what I did, and in subtle ways, I will never be the same person as the one who began that trek. I'll always keep the courage I grew along the way, and if I ever return to those remote islands and mangrove forests, I won't feel the same trepidation the second time around.

So let's go on a journey, shall we? Let's have an adventure! Let's become truly alive for once! Let's explore one of the most notable sources of happiness possible: courage and determination. Let's find out where it will lead us next.

If you try and fail, then reconsider, because *you did not fail!* If you struck out boldly, even for only a moment, then you exercised your courage, and that in itself may be the most important victory of all, because as your courage grows stronger and steadier, your fears will recede and you will conquer your worst enemy. You will utterly disarm your most dreadful fears. You will vanquish your most intense barrier to living happily ever after.

Ponder & Discuss

1. List three of the fears which keep you from doing and getting and being what you want. Write them down, as always.
2. Choose one of those fears, then make a plan, chart a course, and decide how you will face it. You can outline a single baby step, three bold giant steps, or sprint headlong into the storm, that's totally up to you.
3. Discuss your plan with someone if you need moral support or to commit yourself to action - someone who will hold you accountable.

Take Action

1. Execute your plan, one step at a time, and take notes on how your courage and confidence grow along the way.

In Other Words

"A ship in the harbor is safe, but that is not what ships are built for." – John A Shedd

"Those who dare to fail miserably can achieve greatly." – John F. Kennedy

"A coward dies a thousand times before his death, but the valiant taste of death but once. It seems to me most strange that men should fear, seeing that death, a necessary end, will come when it will come." - William Shakespeare

"One of the most tragic things I know about human nature is that all of us tend to put off living. We are all dreaming of some magical rose garden over the horizon instead of enjoying the roses that are blooming outside our windows today." – Dale Carnegie

"I have learned over the years that when one's mind is made up, this diminishes fear; knowing what must be done does away with fear." -Rosa Parks

Chapter 25: Judge and Jury

One of the most dangerous threats to your happiness is to ask yourself, "Am I happy?" This inquiry instantly turns your brain into a courtroom where evidence for and against gets presented, and the debate itself alters the outcome.

"On one hand," you may reason, "it's a beautiful day, I'm healthy, and I feel good." Great! It sounds like you're happy!

"But on the other," you continue, "I have to go back to work tomorrow, I'm not attractive enough to make everyone fall instantly in love with me, and I only got six likes on my last social media post." Darn, maybe you're not so happy after all.

"But overall, sure, I'm relatively happy," you assert.

"Objection!" cries the prosecution. "You're a loser! Someone honked at you in traffic this morning - they hate you! You made a mistake, therefore you *are* a mistake, and your kitchen's a mess! The world is a worse place because you're in it, and you'll never amount to anything!"

Whoa, that's harsh!

"But it *might* be true!" the prosecution continues. "There's at least a 1% chance that there's a sliver of truth to it!"

In the battle between happy and unhappy states, negative thoughts have an advantage over positive ones, because negatives are problems, and problems might be dangerous, and your brain is wired to protect you from dangers, so it focuses on them more than on positives, which are pleasant and pretty but not crucial for your survival.

Furthermore, focusing on negatives makes them appear more true, even though that's not an accurate way to evaluate facts *at all*.

If you ever find yourself caught in the downward spiral of negative thinking, remind yourself that happiness is nothing more than a state, and that state depends primarily on your subjective reaction to what you're doing or being, or to your circumstances, and your world doesn't have to be perfect for you to feel happy. If it did, nobody would ever be happy, or at least not for long.

You are the sole judge and jury in this case, if you allow yourself to be, and if you find even a spark of happiness inside and focus on that, then you can rule that you are, in fact, happy, and that will be the truth. Case closed! End of story! Happy until proven otherwise!

While working in Arkansas last winter, I ran across the Mississippi River one rainy night (on a bridge, of course). About half way across, I stopped just before the state line, then took a single step forward, and found myself in Tennessee. I stepped backward and returned to Arkansas once again.

One moment I was in one state, and in the next instant, with only the barest minimal effort, I was in another. I easily crossed the line with only the slightest change in physical reality.

That's how simple it is to change your state. Once you grasp onto a happy thought and let it fill your consciousness, pushing away most of the unhappy ones, you are, in reality, in that instant, happy.

You don't have to feel *perfectly* happy. You don't have to feel utterly *blissful*, or about to erupt in Disney-esque song and dance with all of nature humming the backup melodies. All you need is a single spark of happiness, and that counts. You are officially happy.

Whether or not you're strong enough to hold onto that conviction of happiness, whether you can't maintain it for more than a moment, is irrelevant. Right now, in this split second, you are happy. The more you accept this truth, the easier it becomes to believe it and feel it.

I encourage you to accept this fact. Enter it into evidence as exhibit A. Let yourself receive any small victory you can achieve, because winning such small battles is the way to rebuild your entire life for the better, one tiny triumph at a time.

Making yourself become happy is worth a point, and accepting that you're happy earns another. Every minute you maintain that state adds another number to the scoreboard, and there's no opposing team you must outscore. It's just you, so continue racking up those points.

You don't win the war of happiness by getting rich and never having to work again. You don't win it by growing older or looking younger, by losing weight or gaining experience, or by any such outward measurement.

Sure, while everything goes your way, you may feel fantastic! There's nothing wrong with that, and I wish it upon you in abundance. But if you want to guarantee eternal happiness, you must learn to hold onto it even when you find outside circumstances less supportive.

Practice the ultimate, self-contained happiness skill right now by conjuring up the feeling of happiness, then holding onto it. You don't need a reason. Don't talk yourself into it or do anything enjoyable, just say, "Hey, happiness, come over here for a minute," and welcome it into your brain. Throw an arm around its shoulder and walk forward together.

Once you succeed at that, practice accepting the fact that you have placed yourself in a state of happiness and that you are, in fact, right now, happy.

You are both judge and jury of your own happiness, and here's what makes that so crucially important: the more often you admit that you're happy, the more evidence you present and accept to make your case, the more often you rule in your favor, the more you will build your new norm, your new balance point, the more your subconscious will believe in and support your happiness, and the more readily and effortlessly you will find it reflected in your perceptions and physical reality.

Ponder & Discuss

1. How self-critical are you? Why? How much does that affect your happiness and productivity? How does it affect your ability to connect with and enjoy others, and for them to

enjoy you?
2. Do you view your circumstances as mostly supportive or draining? Would it be possible to make your outlook more positive? How much would that affect your quality of life?

Take Action

1. Conduct the experiment outlined above by summoning happiness from thin air, then holding it for as long as you can. How long *can* you hold onto it? Does it get easier with practice?
2. Try this experiment with someone else and observe whether you find it easier or harder in their company. Why might that be?

In Other Words

"We fight our most brutal battles entirely within the deepest confines of our own minds in a place where nobody else, however compassionate or well-meaning, can come close to reaching. Friends can cheer you on, people who love you can show their concern and affection constantly… in the end, it doesn't matter, you're still alone. If you can't save yourself, it can't be saved. I wish I'd realized this sooner, it would've saved me years of grief." – Kirt Manwaring

"I found in my research that the biggest reason people aren't more self-compassionate is that they are afraid they'll become self-indulgent. They believe self-criticism is what keeps them in line. Most people have gotten it wrong because our culture says being hard on yourself is the way to be." – Kristen Neff

Chapter 26: The Narrow Now

I know two ways to make yourself feel fully present. The first is to sit down in a quiet place, fold your legs into lotus position, and meditate. Focus on your breath and let random thoughts float away into outer space.

The second method is the one I chose this afternoon, and the reason I find myself flying down a narrow dirt path cut across a rugged mountainside, my bicycle clattering over rocks and roots along the winding trail, letting gravity have its way with me, tugging the wheels round and round with only minimal effort on my part, and resisting the urge to reach for the brakes until I can no longer help it, until my survival instinct kicks in and overrides my determination to drive every thought but the split second immediately before me from my mind.

I think of wise old Lao Tzu's quote about living in the present when he said that if you're depressed, then you're focusing on the past. If anxious, you're focused on the future. Living in the present frees you from fear and brings peace.

Perhaps Lao Tzu wasn't quite as wise as everyone gives him credit for. At the very least, he didn't take mountain biking into account, because right now I feel both completely present and utterly afraid.

Rocks and gravel crunch below my tires, limestone outcroppings fly by in a blur, and scrub oak sometimes reaches out its tiny branches, scraping my shins and bringing a trace of red to the surface, giving me a small hint of what the cost would be of losing control and crashing into them.

I reach out a finger on each hand and squeeze the brakes, bringing the bike back into control, the speed back within my comfort zone, and now I feel...alive! Alert. Awake. Invigorated. The fear I felt was purifying, not paralyzing; stimulating, not stagnating.

I peel my eyes from the trail long enough to take quick glances at the world around me - the late afternoon sun falling through a pale blue sky. The small, green leaves just beginning to turn to bright red and yellow fire. The rocky trail weaving beautifully around the mountain's smooth or jagged contours. Everything is utterly beautiful, and there is nowhere I would rather be.

Where do you spend most of your days? I'm not referring to your home or school or office or factory. I'm asking about your mind. How often is it right there with you, or how often does it only check in with you occasionally, paying attention primarily to daydreams or memories or imaginary events and conversations?

Daydreaming has its value, and you can often find plenty of good, quality happiness there. But you must also develop the ability to stay present if you hope to extract the best results and happiness from real world events, situations, and relationships.

Being fully present is rarely more crucial than when conversing with people who matter, or who you want to matter. If your attention is divided by random feelings or planning whatever you want to say next, people will sense it, and that will rob you both of the full satisfaction of connection.

I remember meeting Natalie, one of my favorite friends of all time, who started out as my university student. She had an interesting, uncommon light about her, and I wanted to understand where that light came from.

So whenever she spoke, I paid as much attention to that light as to whatever she was saying, hoping that comprehension would eventually dawn on me.

I made sure to pay attention to my other students as well so no one would notice.

I can't say that I ever figured it out, but we became friends and I later learned what she was thinking at the time. She noted my steady eye contact and full openness and attention, and briefly wondered if it meant anything special about her. But then she watched how I interacted with her fellow students and concluded that I looked at everyone the same way.

"You don't make it about yourself," she explained when we went for a drive the next summer, "you make it about the other person."

She implied that I made people feel seen, and that made them feel appreciated, valued and safe. That, in turn, made them willing to participate in class discussion, which contributed to the fact that we never took a single break during our two-and-a-half-hour class periods, and everyone often looked surprised that the time had flown by so quickly when class ended.

If you'd like to foster a more rewarding, engaging atmosphere in your life and develop higher-quality connections with others, then learn to wake up to the present moment more often. Practice paying closer attention.

Learn to not let other thoughts and feelings distract you from the precise moment in which you find yourself. Strive to live in the narrow now and nowhere else, at least during the moments that matter.

If you don't, then you risk letting life pass by like a dream, and once it's over, you may wonder why you missed the whole thing.

Ponder & Discuss

1. List two or three times when you've felt happy recently, and recall where your mind was. Were you fully present and engaged, or otherwise?
2. Recall several recent conversations you've shared with others. How present were you at the time? How present were they? What difference did that make?
3. Who do you know who often seems present? How can you tell? How does that seem to influence their happiness?

Take Action

1. Take a walk somewhere and do your best to remain perfectly present, absolutely aware of your current surroundings. Feel your body move and take in your surroundings without getting distracted by other thoughts. See how long you can maintain that focus, and how it influences your mood.
2. Have a conversation and *listen* closely to the other person. Avoid the urge to prepare your next comment. Note how this changes the quality of your connection.
3. Choose a thought - any thought, every thought's a winner! - and test your ability to focus. You may choose a problem you wish to solve or a concept or trait you'd like to ponder, learn, and integrate.

   Get a pen and paper, then set a countdown timer for four minutes on your phone and press go. Every time you catch your mind wandering, make a mark on the page.

   Score yourself like golf - the lower the score, the better you did. If you only lose focus three or four times, you're doing well above average. If your mind drifts eight or ten or more times, you could definitely use more practice.

In Other Words

"The only thing you have to heal is the present thought. Get that right and the whole picture will change into one of harmony and joy." – Eckhart Tolle

"Yesterday is already a dream and tomorrow is only a vision. But today, well-lived, makes every yesterday a dream of happiness and every tomorrow a vision of hope." – Kalidasa

"Love is a present activity only, the man who does not manifest love in the present has not love." – Tolstoy

Chapter 27: Live in the Past

I got hired to teach English at Utah Valley University on the third day of class after another teacher quit. I scrambled to assemble a simple syllabus based on one I used as a teaching assistant while earning my masters degree, and showed up at school the next morning feeling ready to go.

I still remember walking into my second classroom. Becca sat in the third row and her face was a portrait of perfect boredom.

"Hi, everyone," I began. "I'm Shaun Roundy, and I'll be taking over your class for the rest of the semester. You can call me Shaun, and I'd like to begin by listing everything you hate about English classes."

There was no use denying that writing is not everyone's favorite subject. By the time students reach college, they've BSed their way through hundreds of pages of busywork, they've received grades they didn't understand when they thought they deserved better, they've been given contradictory instructions by one teacher or another, and even if all that wasn't true, most students are only interested in investing the least possible effort to earn an A. They don't expect all this to apply to their real lives any more than the quadratic formula.

"Let's start with this one," I said, pointing to one of the items I had listed on the board. "Is it okay or not to use the word 'I' when writing a paper?"

I drew a quick continuum on the board with an F at one end, and a C at the other, then scrawled an X near the F end. "If you're writing a paper here," I explained, you should generally not use the word 'I'. If you write a paper here," I continued, while drawing another X near the other side," it's not only okay, it's expected."

I glanced at my students to see if I had their attention and if any of them seemed to be catching on. "Can anyone tell me what the F and the C stand for?" I asked.

Seconds passed as students processed the question or gathered up the courage to answer. I waited.

A hand rose from near the back, and I pointed at the boy who it belonged to. "What's your name?" I asked.

"Sam."

"What do you think, Sam? What do F and C stand for?"

"Is the F for formal?"

"Correct!" I replied, stabbing the air with my dry erase marker for punctuation.

"And the C is for casual?" Leslie volunteered, speaking up as she raised her hand.

"Right!" I confirmed. "Formal writing attempts to remain as objective as possible, and one way it does so is by eliminating the subjective 'I' whenever possible, even though that's not nearly as effective as people used to believe."

Class continued, and I remember Becca's face about half way through the hour. Her eyebrows were raised and she looked surprised and hesitant. She looked like she wasn't sure what was going on and didn't know what to think about the way class was turning out.

We finished clearing up the reasons to hate English and reviewed the syllabus, explaining each assignment and what they could expect to learn from it. I cracked a few jokes as we went along, and by the time we finished, it no longer felt like day one of class. Students were engaged and participating, and I was enjoying myself immensely.

And Becca? It looked like she had made up her mind. She was grinning from ear to ear; happily, shamelessly enjoying English class.

Why do I share this story? Because many moments from my teaching career (though not so much the endless grading part) are among my most cherished memories. Watching students not only learn, but learn to love learning. Observing them participate and support each other, and become invested in their paper assignments as if they could change the world. Walking out of a classroom and not recalling what I said, but remembering the faces of everyone laughing heartily.

The past is the past, and little of it remains besides relationships and memories, or perhaps a few dollars in your bank account, or debts accruing interest on your credit card bill.

Since it's over and gone, the past only serves two useful purposes - to learn from and to enjoy.

If you have unpleasant memories from the past, and if you've already learned your lessons from them, then do not dwell there. It can only drain your happiness now and poison the future.

In fact, since you've extracted all the value you can from them, perhaps it's time to alter them a little. Go ahead and add an imaginary happy ending. It doesn't change the past, but it changes your mind. Even when you know better, it drains the poison from the memory to replay a better version of it so it can stop tormenting you.

Who's to say you can't? Well, it's not up to them! Do it anyway.

And your pleasant memories? Go ahead and enjoy them, celebrate them, even! That's what they're good for.

But heed this one warning: do not compare them to the present too much, not if you imagine that you had it better then. Not if remembering the good then brings you sorrow and suffering now.

Instead, get busy constructing a new past by generating more happy memories today. It's like the invaluable lesson from my favorite quote by Wendell Barry:

> "The only way to change the past is to replace it with something better."

If someone accuses you of bragging when you celebrate a memory, just shake your head and say, "I didn't figure you for a member of the Ego Police," then ask them to share a good memory and show them how to properly celebrate others' good fortune.

Yes, go ahead and enjoy the past. Visit often if you like. Just don't stay there forever, but return to the present renewed, encouraged, and enthusiastically determined to continue constructing more and more and more happy memories to enjoy in days to come.

WORKSHOP

Ponder & Discuss

1. List at least three of your favorite memories. Why do you enjoy them? What do they reveal about who you are and what you're worth?
2. Share a memory with someone who will celebrate it with you, then be thoughtful and ask them to share a memory so you can return the favor.
3. List one unpleasant memory. What have you learned from it? How has that experience made you a better person today?

Take Action

1. Rewrite history. Take an unpleasant memory which you no

longer need and inject it with happier thoughts and images. Remember yourself as being wiser and braver. Remember others as being kinder. Imagine the happiest ending you can possibly invent. Let these images play through your mind for a little while, then notice how differently you feel about the memory.

In Other Words

"That which is bitter to endure may be sweet to remember." – Thomas Fuller

"The things we remember best are those better forgotten." – Baltasar Gracian

Chapter 28: Clarity

The Rio Lindo drops 140' over the Pulhapanzak waterfall (which is only 48 feet shy of Niagara), then continues as a deep, green river flowing through central Honduras. My friend who lived nearby led me through the dripping-wet cave system below the falls, then to a fifty-foot cliff just downstream. Now I stood atop the cliff and stared down into the current.

I felt a touch of fear and a thrill of excitement as a few local boys threw themselves off the cliff and into the river. I couldn't wait to take my turn. I knew the water was deep enough, and clear of any rocks or branches below the surface to smash my bones against or impale me, so why would I worry?

Once the last boy surfaced and swam toward shore, I took three quick steps toward the edge and leapt into the air. There could be no turning back now!

Wind whipped through my hair and whistled past my ears as I fell and fell and fell, until I struck the river's surface and the wind whipping around my body was replaced by thick, cool water, the sound of bubbles, and the muffled roar of the river.

Fifteen feet underwater, my body slowed to a stop, and before taking my first strokes back toward the surface, it dawned on me that I could open my eyes.

I had grown up wearing contact lenses which I occasionally lost while swimming or crashing on waterskis, so I had learned to close my eyelids tightly when underwater, but my recent LASIK surgery changed all that. Now I had nothing to lose, and therefore nothing to fear by opening my lids.

I opened my eyes, tilted my head back, and looked up through the clear river. Even now, many years later, I still vividly recall the beautiful green water sloshing high above my head.

I paused for several moments just to watch while the current carried me downstream, and only the vacuum forming in my lungs persuaded me to return to the surface and swim back to shore.

If you asked me to choose the best two or three dozen vignettes from my life - brief, memorable moments of beauty, fun, meaning and happiness, I would certainly list jumping off that cliff and opening my eyes underwater among them, and it was only made possible because I dared to leap away from solid ground.

What most people need most if they want to become happier

is emotional LASIK surgery. They need their vision corrected - not the physical kind, but the imaginary. They look out at the world and feel afraid. They see imaginary dangers that don't actually exist. They perceive overwhelming risks in the most innocuous opportunities when in reality they have nothing at all to lose.

Uncomfortable feelings well up inside - pressures and anxieties, and those sensations make the fear feel real.

Such false fears not only prevent people from pursuing their dreams, but stand in the way of enjoying normal everyday opportunities to smile, laugh, relax, connect, express themselves, and enjoy the passing hours as life flows along its beautiful, lively, sloshing course downstream along the river of time.

Is it not perfectly obvious how much better it would be to take three steps forward, jump, *go for it,* live your dreams, open your eyes, and let life fall into place around you, pressing up against your skin, and looking more beautiful than ever from the center of the current, rather than standing timidly on the shore as if you were only a passive observer of life? A mere tourist?

Maybe not every time, but sometimes! And how can you judge whether that time should be *this* time if you've never even tried and have no experience of living more fully and watching life turn out happier and better for it?

If this suggestion frightens you, then good for you! That shows that you're considering taking a chance and living more fully. Keep on considering it until you select a worthy cliff to jump off and leap into mid-air, the wind whipping through your hair, gleefully shouting *"Geronimo!!!"* all the way down to your bliss.

Take Action

Take a safe risk and discover that it's not so difficult nor dangerous after all, and that you can live your life more freely than ever before. You can make it a single baby step or a pair of giant strides you've always wanted to take. It needn't be a physical risk, though safe physical risks are often the quickest to learn from.

Let's break this into helpful steps:

1. Identify a safe risk you could take, but that you hesitate due to fear, doubt, or discomfort, and that would add to your

happiness if you followed through.
2. Jot down the worst that could likely come from trying it, just to make sure it's actually safe.
3. Write down what would most likely happen, and the best that could happen. Observe others doing the same thing and see how well it turns out for them.
4. If you need more time to prepare, then imagine yourself doing it - boldly, bravely, expertly, until it grows more comfortable. It may feel more exciting to leap before you're completely ready, before it feels easy, but on the other hand, you may enjoy it more if you feel relaxed and ready.
5. Do it. Try it. A little at a time or all at once. Take a deep breath, step forward, and let your body fall into the moment with no chance of turning back.

Ponder & Discuss
1. As soon as you've taken an actual risk and survived it, discuss this process and experience with others.

In Other Words

"When you know who you are; when your mission is clear and you burn with the inner fire of unbreakable will; no cold can touch your heart; no deluge can dampen your purpose. You know that you are alive." – Chief Seattle

"Hell begins on the day when God grants us a clear vision of all that we might have achieved, of all the gifts which we have wasted, of all that we might have done which we did not do." – Gian-Carlo Menotti

Chapter 29: True Princess

In "The Princess and the Pea," a girl sleeps on a tall stack of soft mattresses, but below the bottom mattress lies a single green pea. In the morning, the girl is bruised black and blue, and reports that she was so uncomfortable that she couldn't sleep a wink, and that's how they prove she must be a true princess.

I don't understand why anyone would find such daintiness appealing, and - worse - the world is packed with such princesses today.

If you don't believe me, find a beautiful, inspiring, heroic, or otherwise commendable video on YouTube, then scan through the comments to find the critics and haters. It won't take long.

Haters gonna hate. Critics look for the negative and unfailingly find it, while turning a blind eye to much of the positive and commendable that the world generously offers them.

It's as if they feel entitled to expect the world to be perfect, and not only perfect, but *their* brand of perfect. As if they have the *right*, dammit!, for everyone to agree with the first thought that pops into their head, and behave reasonably and decently, exactly the way they define it.

Even if everyone did, however, the critic would still find something to complain about.

What's most likely going on in their heads and hearts is that they're experiencing negative emotions - fear, loneliness, unworthiness, hurt, confusion, frustration, etc. - and they're trying to discharge those feelings onto others, as if spewing them with words could get rid of them once and for all.

But it doesn't work that way. Setting the rest of the world on fire won't extinguish the flames of your own personal hell, it only makes them burn higher and hotter.

We're all guilty of this sort of behavior to some extent. If you examine yourself closely, you may discover that you're a bit of a princess yourself. How often, and to what extent, do you get hung up on the negatives in your life (or others'), and allow dissatisfaction and frustration to ruin your day?

Maybe you rarely criticize others, but do you treat yourself as generously? Or do you often dwell more on your minor flaws (even the ones that nobody else in the whole wide world ever notices) than your positive traits?

Most people are surrounded by more opportunity, blessings, beauty, and comfort than ever before available to the human race, yet they choose to focus on a tiny pea - any detectable or imaginary imperfection.

You probably don't consciously choose to focus on the negative. In fact, it's not entirely your fault. Your subconscious brain is wired to identify problems and resolve them - it's part of your survival instinct. If all is well, then that's nice, but you can ignore it and it won't kill you.

Then again, the vast majority of modern negatives won't kill you, either. Ignore them, and the only result will be increased peace and happiness.

That's why it's up to your conscious mind to actively choose a more positive focus. Consciously scan for uplifting things. If you want to feel happier, that's how you get there.

Do not make excuses. Do not delay! Begin scanning your surrounding world for good immediately and do so with gusto and enthusiasm!

If you need more convincing, ask yourself how much paying attention to the non-lethal negatives that hold your attention, getting frustrated or angry or indignant or depressed helps the situation. Probably not much, right? In fact, it usually makes things worse.

Secondly, how much does it undermine your happiness? The answer could be: *a lot!* Is it worth continuing down that ugly road? Or would you rather change course as quickly as possible?

Changing your life requires you to alter your thoughts and perceptions, your behaviors and habits, and that can take time, so remain patient while you sample new thoughts and break down old habits.

I'm not asking you to sugarcoat anything. I'm not asking you to go into denial of all the world's flaws and see everything only through rose-colored glasses.

Real, serious problems abound and they still require solving, but you would be a fool to let them dominate your every waking thought.

I'm only asking you to stop crap coating everything you see and justifying yourself by claiming to be a "realist."

May I suggest a compromise: divide your time. If something

bothers you, then choose something you can do to improve the situation and schedule time for that - as much or as little as you choose.

The rest of the time, let it go! Forget about it for a while. And live a happier life as a result - which, by the way, has been demonstrated repeatedly as a highly effective way to turn yourself into a better problem solver.

There ya go. Win-win. If you truly are a realist, and if you truly want to solve problems and make the world better, then you can't turn down this request.

Bye, bye, true princess. Say hello to true nobility and grace.

Ponder & Discuss

1. List three of your pet peeves. Are you being too picky and negative about them? What would happen if you took a deep breath and tried to forget about them or accept them as they are?
2. Does it do any good to complain about imperfections and focus on the negative? Does it do any harm? How much does it affect your happiness? How much does it affect others'?

Take Action

1. Look around you and find something beautiful. Anything at all! Stare at it for a while and allow yourself to enjoy the way it makes you feel, and the way it alters your state. If you find flaws, forgive them immediately, and turn back to appreciating the beauty.

   Note how this alters your state, and whether you like the new state better.
2. Look around and find something (or someone) you dislike - the more you hate it the better. Now list as many positive attributes as possible about that item (or person), and allow yourself to appreciate them.

   Write a paragraph about how it would change your life to make this a habit? What would happen if everyone tried this more often?

In Other Words

"The greatest degree of inner tranquility comes from the development of love and compassion. The more we care for the happiness of others, the greater is our own sense of well-being."- Tenzin Gyatso, 14th Dalai Lama

"Had we ourselves no faults, we should find less pleasure discovering them in others." – Francois de La Rochefoucauld

"A modest man often seems conceited because he is delighted with what he has done, thinking is better than anything of which he believed himself capable, whereas the conceited man is inclined to express dissatisfaction with his performances, thinking them unworthy of his genius." – Hesketh Pearson

"The poorest way to face life is to face it with a sneer. There are many men who feel a kind of twister pride in cynicism; there are many who confine themselves to criticism of the way others do what they themselves dare not even attempt." – Theodore Roosevelt

"There is only one way to avoid criticism: do nothing, say nothing, and be nothing." – Aristotle

"You have been criticizing yourself for years, and it hasn't worked. Try approving of yourself and see what happens." – Louise L. Hay

Chapter 30: Get What You Give

As the clock started and the basketball game began, the entire crowd calmly rose to their feet and started clapping. Not the random, raucous cheering that follows a goal or good play, but a steady, unified rhythm that filled the arena - clap! Clap! Clap! Clap! Clap!

This clapping would continue until the home team scored their first point of the game, when the cheers and applause would burst forth with renewed vigor and enough volume to make children cover their ears for protection.

The first point would also signal the moment for hundreds of fans to throw rolls of toilet paper toward the center of the floor, filling the air with white streamers, halting the game until wide brooms swept the floor clean, and earning a technical foul to the home team which allowed the visitors to score a point, but it was worth it.

This was my school, my team, and tonight my university not only played our biggest rival, but ESPN was streaming the game live to a national audience. I felt proud when watching the reruns of that first point and seeing the entire arena turn white with streamers immediately afterward.

By the end of the night, we would make history, with the then-highest-scoring game ever in college basketball - 143 to 144 in triple overtime, with us losing by a single point.

Our school's arena is famously difficult for the visiting team to play in due to the non-stop noise from the fans, who more than once have tipped the balance in our favor.

I've attended several NBA games where fans watch calmly, for the most part, right up until the last five or ten minutes, when they finally stand up and become consistently loud and worked up, which makes the final minutes exciting, but the rest of the game... just okay.

This is the sort of heart and enthusiasm which often makes college sports so much more fun to watch than professional games, even when the pros are exponentially better athletes.

If you've attended any other sort of performance - whether a play or concert or otherwise, you may have noticed that when the audience shows their appreciation, when they feed energy to the players, then the performers respond with a more energized, engaging, and inspiring performance. The audience helps to bring them alive.

Conversely, I once sat in the studio audience for the recording of a television sitcom in Los Angeles in which a friend of a friend was an actor, and the audience just wasn't that into it. We didn't cheer or laugh much. We mostly just sat and watched, passively waiting to be entertained.

The most famous actor in the production turned to us several times and commented on the fact - she could feel the lack of audience support and it seemed to irritate her.

Sorry. I should have tried harder.

Now think about your life and your behavior - what type of energy do you invest in the people or "players" around you? How often do you stand up and cheer for your family, friends, and schoolmates or coworkers? What would happen if you did so more often? How would that enhance their performance, and how might they respond more positively to you?

How often do others invest in you by spending time together, paying attention to your thoughts and needs, and taking genuine interest in your struggles and triumphs? How does it make you feel when they do? How does it affect your outlook, hope and happiness when they don't?

One benefit to cheering for others is that it earns you the right to celebrate and enjoy their victories. It's like watching a movie where the actor doesn't even know you exist (and, quite possibly, doesn't care that you do), yet your spirits soar as you watch them face daunting challenges with courage and overcome impossible odds. It's hardly about them anymore, your experience is all about you.

Note that you don't need to "belong" to someone in order to cheer them on. Just like in sports, a fan who has never set foot east of the Mississippi can still choose a New York team as "theirs," while a native New Yorker who has never traveled beyond New Jersey may root for a team from Texas or California.

Celebrating others is not the only way to invest more energy into your life and reap the returns. Thanks to COVID-19, I've been practicing social distancing by working from home for the last several months. I join my team for a call every morning and afternoon, and I've gotten in the habit of shouting "ALOHA!!!" when I first connect.

It's not that I always feel that exuberant, but I immediately noticed that it makes me feel more so. It's good for me, and, I suspect, for whoever was already connected when I join.

The point of these stories is that you get what you give, and whatever you give often returns to you amplified by others' reactions.

That's the point of this entire book, in fact, which points out many ways you can give and receive happiness.

So don't just act, act with enthusiasm! Speak up loudly (when appropriate)! Pour yourself into your life heart and soul, and watch how it immediately or eventually comes back to you in similar fashion.

There's no limit on how much of yourself you invest into every moment, because every passing moment consumes every single particle that exists in the entire universe all at once anyway, then spits it back out into the next moment.

Pour a little in, and you'll get a little back. Pour everything in, and your richest possible life will be poured back out, filling your cup to overflowing.

Ponder & Discuss
1. List recent actions which you've performed both enthusiastically and lacklusterly. How much did you enjoy each one? How much did enthusiasm (or lack thereof) affect your enjoyment?
2. List something that someone else did energetically. Did you find their liveliness contagious? Would you like to live your life more like them? Why or why not?

Take Action
1. Pick an appropriate occasion and shout "Aloha!" Note whether it boosts your mood, and if it doesn't, try again. Do your best to let it work.

In Other Words

> "Three Rules for Success:
> 1. Start Now.
> 2. Do it Flamboyantly.

3. No Exceptions."
– William James (paraphrased)

"Enthusiasm is the yeast that makes your hopes shine to the stars. Enthusiasm is the sparkle in your eyes, the swing in your gait. The grip of your hand, the irresistible surge of will and energy to execute your ideas." -Henry Ford

"The worst bankrupt in the world is the person who has lost his or her enthusiasm. Let one lose everything but enthusiasm and that person will again come through to success." – H.W. Arnold

"If I were to wish for anything, I should not wish for wealth and power, but for the passionate sense of what might be, for the eye which, ever young and ardent, sees the possible. Pleasure disappoints, possibility never. And what wine is so sparkling, what so fragrant, what so intoxicating as possibility." – Soren Kierkegaard

To Be Continued...

My sister Nicole has a 4x4' board full of colorful blue, red and white ribbons from her gymnastics career, and I would often pick her up after practice before she was old enough to drive.

I found one of her teammates rather attractive, which may have contributed to the fact that I sometimes arrived early, and would sit in the stands and watch them finish up. Heather had dark brown hair and matching eyes. She was my age or a year younger and attended the high school to the south, where I had several close friends.

On one hand, I was excited when Nicki told me that Heather had noticed me, too, and thought I was cute.

On the other hand, I was still quite shy, even if it didn't usually show, so it took a bit of courage to ask her out, but I did it anyway.

We went to a movie on Friday night, then enjoyed fries and shakes to give us a chance to talk and get acquainted. I don't know whether to blame my shyness and inability to relax, or whether she was equally shy, but conversation didn't flow very naturally, and after I dropped her off, I didn't think the date went terribly well or that she was at all interested in me.

I went skiing with friends the next day and saw Heather on the slopes from time to time. I wondered if she noticed how well I shredded the moguls below the ski lift as she passed by overhead, and appreciated that she was a fine skier as well, but I pretended not to notice her presence.

When we stopped for lunch in the lodge, Heather and her group of friends sat fifteen feet away down the long table. Her little sister threw French fries at me to get my attention, but I felt too shy to even go over and say hello or ask if I could ski with them for a while.

It should have been so simple! With a few runs together, we surely would have relaxed a little and quite possibly become lasting friends.

The world is so filled with grand opportunities, and I hate thinking about how many I have missed for one reason or another.

But I have since learned better. I have learned to speak up and act, and to ask for what I want, just in case that allows me to get it.

Which brings us to the point of this final chapter.

The point is that this is *not* the final chapter. I have dozens more insightful lessons about catching and keeping happiness, along with engaging stories to illustrate them, in varying stages of readiness for publication.

In other words, it doesn't have to be over between you and me - not if you don't want it to be. I know I don't!

Just give me a sign. If you've enjoyed this book, and if you've found it helpful, and because you can't toss a french fry at me, then instead give it a five-star review on Amazon. Tell your friends and tell the world what you like about *The Happiness Equation* so I can see that there's a demand for more.

Only then can I know that the hours and evenings and weekends and years that I've spent writing it rather than chasing my own happiness in all my favorite ways are worth the sacrifice because they will make someone's world a better and brighter place.

I hope this book has already made a difference in your perspective, behaviors, and outcomes. In other words, I hope you're happier than when you began reading. I hope that upward trend will continue forever, and that your happy glow will spread far and wide.

Heaven knows our world could use more of you shining bravely your happiest, best self.

More books by Shaun Roundy:

Uplifting Fiction
The Art of Heart Christmas Trilogy

Book 1:
Courage, Love and the Meaning of Christmas
Order from Amazon.com:
bit.ly/artheart1

Spencer Cook is searching for the Meaning of Life, but time is running out. He is searching for love, and time is running out. He is frantically searching for a girl, lost somewhere out in a cold winter storm, and time is running out.

Lucky for him, courage changes everything.

Follow Spencer through a magical, whirlwind Christmas vacation full of adventure, romance, and intense personal growth. When you finish, your perspective of Life and Christmas will change forever.

Courage, Love and the Meaning of Christmas provides a complete guide to the Meaning of Life hidden between the lines of a magical, engaging, page-turning, thrilling novel packed with laugh-out-loud, cry-along, and shout-for-joy moments.

The original version of this popular holiday story spent two years in Amazon.com's top 200 rankings and earned a reputation as an engaging and difficult-to-put-down book.

Reader Reviews:

 M. Gordon

I laughed. I cried. The story stuck with me and made me think. I, like Spencer, thought about the meaning of life. As I read this thoughts and the characters wriggled their way into my heart. After I finished, I found these thoughts had blossomed and I will be better for having read this.

 By J. Partridge

I really loved this book. I read it in two nights — practically couldn't put it down. Roundy is a pro in this genre. He really captures the heart of interpersonal interactions and relationships, and mixes in the right amount of suspense and adventure. And he takes a much needed and profound look at the real meaning and purpose of life. An excellent read! (And I'm excited that this story about Spencer is a trilogy!)

 By Samuel Pucketton

This is an awesome book well written and pulls you in as a part of the story. It is real life as he questions what is the real meaning of life. He gets his answers living life with family friends and of course meeting a young lady that shares his dreams and challenging his thoughts dreams and bringing out the best in him. A great read that's hard to put down.

 By P. Poynor "granmama"

I read this book and its sequel, The Perfect Gift, and found both to be thought provoking as well as entertaining. Spencer and Ski seem to be an unlikely pair to engage in friendship, but it works. Spencer has to fight through his insecurities to discover who he really is. That leads him to visit his grandmother earlier than planned and where he meets Annetta. He discovers that his friendship with Annetta brings out the best in him.

Through the course of the two books, Spencer and Ski both discover their best selves. But there are unresolved issues with Annetta. I'm eager to read the last book in the trilogy.

Book 2:
The Perfect Gift
Order from Amazon.com:
bit.ly/artheart2

The Perfect Gift is the long-awaited sequel to *Courage, Love and the meaning of Christmas*. The story picks up 11 months later as the next Christmas rolls around. Much has changed for Spencer and friends, but not nearly as much as is about to!

You will be surprised. It's not what you were expecting. Then you'll be surprised again and again and again. Sometimes pleasantly, sometimes...well, you'll find out. Life is not always easy. How will you respond when things don't go as planned – for better or for worse?

The Perfect Gift wraps up some loose ends from *Courage, Love and the Meaning of Christmas*, while some of your favorite characters from book one return to play in new and surprising ways.

And we'll warn you, *The Perfect Gift* has even more unpredictable plot twists that will keep you guessing start to finish. (Hint: you'll never guess what happens!)

You'll also get a healthy dose of new insights – this time, instead of courage, love, and the meaning of life, you'll learn about change, choice, and miracles.

You will be surprised. It's more than you're expecting.

If you enjoyed *Courage, Love and the Meaning of Christmas*, you'll again find yourself saying "This book describes my life!"

Reader Reviews:

☆☆☆☆☆ By Inez

Knew I would love this book. Just as I did the first one. Was sad when I finished and now have to wait for the third book to be released... this series is one of the best I have read.. and I've read tons. What can I say, I'm a bookworm,  and love a heartwarming romance story.

☆☆☆☆☆ By Barb

I am not one to post reviews……but I love this series of books so much that I am leaving a review my first time. If you don't get these books, you are missing out on a wonderfully well written book with lots of love and lots of emotions. I can't express enough how much I love Shaun's books!!! LOVED IT

 By lizzy

I got this book from my daughter and couldn't wait to read it. I loved the first one and the second was just as good. I can't wait for the next one. If the author wasn't such a good professor I would suggest that he quit his day job. Great book for all ages. Happiness

Book 3:
The Art of Heart
Order from Amazon.com:
bit.ly/artheart

The Art of Heart brings an exciting and adventurous conclusion to Spencer's quest for love, meaning, and happiness in *Courage, Love and the meaning of Christmas* and *The Perfect Gift*.

A few days before Christmas, he gets a phone call that could change his life. The next day, he catches a plane to join an expedition up the tallest mountain in the continental US, but that's not why he goes.

He goes because, for the first time in a long time, he may get another shot at happiness. He goes because even a long shot is better than no shot at all.

Never give up. From the highest of highs to the lowest lows, there is always hope.

This 268-page conclusion to the trilogy packs in plenty more adventure, insights, romance, plot twists, lively dialogue, and engaging character arcs to carry the reader to its engaging conclusion, while keeping you guessing right up to the last page!

Reader Reviews:
☆☆☆☆☆ By Char Mc

I just finished the last book of Shaun Roundy's *Courage, Love and the Meaning of Christmas* trilogy, which I LOVED! Never has there been a book I've read that prompted me to ponder such things so deeply, as we see the main character do throughout the series.

This is such an insightful trilogy and I enjoyed the journey. You fall in love with the characters and by the last book, it'll leave you not wanting it to end.

☆☆☆☆☆ By Kimon

When I read the first two books in this series, I couldn't wait to dive into this third and final book. However, it was a long time coming…..but so worth the wait.

Shaun has a way of writing that is simple yet compelling. The characters are real and the story line is believable. It was fun to go to the mountain and explore nature and the beauty of friendship. Well worth the read.

This. a vampire cure for forever
Order from Amazon.com:
bit.ly/thisvampire

This. has earned high praise from several reviewers for its engaging plot, depth of characterization, useful insights, and more.

The protagonist, Kayla Porter, made the *Best Female Characters of 2010* list, winning Honorable Mention from YA Vampire Books. For Utah Valley residents, you'll enjoy all the action spread throughout the valley, up the canyon, and on the lake.

When Kayla (not her real name) first told me her story, I thought she was just making it up. "We should turn this into a book!" I told her enthusiastically.

She looked hesitant. "Are you sure?" she asked. "I don't really want everyone to know all this about me." Then it was my turn to look at her in confusion. She peered into my eyes intently for a moment, then broke into a broad grin. "You think I'm making this up," she declared. "But I'm not."

I didn't believe her for a long time, but we went to work on the book just the same. Her ability to recount events in exquisite detail surprised and impressed me, as did the passion in her voice as she spoke of new discoveries and narrow escapes.

Only when the story was nearly finished did she show me that she hadn't been imagining this.

All along, I found that the enhanced abilities of vampires provided the ideal microcosm to explore human potentials and dilemmas of identity, courage, power struggles, loyalty, and love. I thought that's all the story was about. In hindsight, I'm glad I didn't know the truth, as I'm not sure I could have calmed down enough to write the story.

The Characters:

Kayla Porter

Kayla begins as just another shy girl with an impossible crush. When the door of opportunity opens, she steps bravely through. Would she do so if she could see what waits on the other side?

The story is told from Kayla's perspective, and she does a fantastic job of not only relating all the action in vivid detail, but also of painting the world with her profound perspective and insights that help make sense of the challenges that she and others face as the plot flies along.

"Life is not what you think," she says in chapter one, and true to her word, this surprising, suspenseful, unforgettable vampire book will suck you in and keep you guessing what happens next from start to finish, then haunt your dreams. Perhaps she was destined for adventure or tragedy all along – it was, after all, in her blood.

Melissa Clayton

Melissa's spunk and spontaneity quickly endear her to everyone she meets. This is both good and bad. Good for Kayla Porter, who likes her immediately. Bad for Mitch Craven, who does the same – or rather, bad for Melissa and everyone else when she catches his eye.

On the other hand, you may not always appreciate Melissa's reckless impulsiveness. Ethan doesn't. As her brother, he loves her unconditionally, but he can't save her. Who knows? Maybe everything will work out for the best. Or not.

What would you do with eternity? How far would you go to prevent "forever" from ending too soon? What happens when desperate dare-devil strategies don't turn out exactly as planned?

Mitch Craven

Mitch Craven starts strong and becomes practically unstoppable.

The crowds love him, but those who know his heart don't feel the same. Even so, they're darn lucky to have him around!

Will he ever get what he wants? He's used to getting his way and doesn't take disappointment lightly.

Everything goes downhill until someone decides it's time to stop him. Will he get what he deserves? Hard to say. Can everyone live happily ever after with Mitch out of the picture? More importantly, will he stay out of the picture?

Ethan Clayton

Ethan is one of the nicest guys you'll ever meet. Popular and positive, he's quite happy with his life. Sorry, Ethan, but it's about to get shaken up! He loves his sister, and it's a good thing, because she certainly tries his patience with all the trouble she attracts.

In most cases, Ethan hardly bats an eye, but he never wanted to be a vampire. The idea repulses him. He never wanted to live forever or be different, but it's better than being dead.

And what does he see in Kayla? What's behind that look he gives her, that curious, amused expression when he looks into her eyes? Does he look that way at everyone or is Kayla someone special?

☆☆☆☆☆ By Cieratownsmc

Overall great book! It was such a page-turner that I stayed up and read it all in one day (and night). Quick but good. Although it's a YA novel, you almost don't miss that it doesn't get "steamy". The characters were easy to love and the story was easy to fallow.

☆☆☆☆☆ By Katherine Blazzard

To escape.

To be invincible.

To find lasting love.

To discover friends false and true.

To dream deeply, live intensely, long for a better world.

To conquer your fears and learn to see what others are really made of.

To learn to be comfortable in your own skin and find power hidden deep within. That is what This is about. Is This a story, a tale, a legend? Yes. This is all of those things.

But This is more. Because This is not just the human story. This encompasses Others.

In This we discover what it means to have a perspective shift. To stop fearing the unknown.

To embrace the different.

To defend your friends with a fierce loyalty.

To follow your heart and your bliss.

To become who you want to become.

To see the world how you would like to see it.

To love and be loved in return. In This, the author gently guides the reader to a place where all of This become a reality. Call it fantasy, call it magic, call it make-believe. But after you read This — you too will want to believe as the characters in the book believed, that your world is what you make it. This is what you have been looking for.

 By db

This book targets such a wide audience, sure to please everyone. Like a little romance and flash backs to high school crushes? You'll love it! More into action and adventure and unexpected twists and suspense? Well, you'll love it too!

With two small boys at home, I don't remember when the last time was that I finished a book. This one I couldn't put down! I finished it in 2 days! With great character development and wonderful details and descriptions it's easy to follow, and too easy to get engulfed by. Yes, it's a vampire book, but just like Kayla says in the beginning, it's not what you're thinking. But it's not just a story either. Full of wisdom and insights, this book isn't just for teens or an empty read.

 By J. Partridge

This. is another suspenseful, insightful, and thoroughly enjoyable story by Shaun Roundy. Reading it produced the kind of feel-good and inspiring experience that I've come to expect reading his work.

I have to say that Chapter 11, "BFF," was probably the best essay I've ever read about being oneself and not giving in to peer pressure or "petty insecurities," as Roundy puts it. Being confident with the person you are, and not letting others opinions affect the way you act, the things you say, the kind of person you know you should be — Roundy nails it on the head and causes you to look closely at your own behaviors, which I really loved.

The vampires in the story are very interesting and quite different than you'd expect, and the story ends with an excellent twist and cliffhanger. A fun and inspiring read, I recommend the book to everyone.

☆☆☆☆☆ By Kirsten

"This" was a surprisingly fun read. Not being a teen anymore didn't discount the fact that it kept me interested in the story. The development of the characters and especially of Mitch was superb.

The story places the heroine in high school and in love. When vampires appear in their lives, danger and excitement and profound experiences ensue. That's really as much as I feel comfortable telling about the story as I don't want to ruin the enjoyment of reading it for yourself!

An inexpensive book that really was fun to read. I'm excited for the sequel!

REAL-LIFE ADVENTURE

75 Search and Rescue Stories: an insider's view of survival, death, and volunteer heroes who tip the balance when things fall apart

Order from Amazon.com:
bit.ly/rescuestories

75 Search and Rescue Stories contains 214 pages of stories and 150 photos of some of the best rescues from the past 12 years on one of the world's best and busiest search and rescue teams.

Author and university writing instructor Shaun Roundy is the ideal person to tell these stories. He is the Utah County Sheriff Search and Rescue Mountain Rescue Team Sergeant and the Mountain Rescue Association Intermountain Region Chair. He has played key roles in hundreds of rescues of all types – trails, cliffs, avalanches, rivers, lakes, caves, and more.

Furthermore, Utah County makes a stunning backdrop for these thrilling stories. It's steep. It's tall. It's extreme in a dozen different ways. Half a million residents can't help getting outside and, sometimes, getting in trouble.

Shaun tells these stories from two perspectives. First, you get a sense of how it feels to be the person who gets in over your head – whether by neglect or merely because the second Law of Nature is entropy: things fall apart. Spend enough time outdoors and it will happen to you.

Next, you learn how it feels to be a professional volunteer rescuer. What motivates them to spend their time and money rescuing strangers on the worst day of their lives, putting everything on the line for people they have never met and will never meet again, 24/7/365, often in the worst possible conditions – and love it?

Throughout it all, vivid descriptions and expressive photographs will keep you glued to the pages, and if you're local, you'll never look at the mountains, canyons, rivers and lakes the same way. That's what happens to SAR members. Every canyon, river, mountain, road and trail has a set of attached memories – some more pleasant than others.

A reviewer for the Mountain Rescue Association wrote, "If you don't have a copy of 75 Search and Rescue Stories in the mail to your address right now, I highly recommend you get one. This is the best rescue book by far that I've ever read."

Reader Reviews:

☆☆☆☆☆ By Lily.cc

This book is well worth twice the price charged, especially given that part of the proceeds are donated to SAR. Divided into quick, engrossing chapters that each tell the story of a SAR operation, it's immensely readable. Some stories will make you laugh, some will leave you in awe.

Shaun Roundy has a fast-paced, light-hearted writing style that never bogs down. Everyone in Utah County should read this before heading to the mountains or the lake; maybe then we'd have fewer people getting ledged out on a cliff in a t-shirt with no gear every month.

I have never required the assistance of SAR, but my brother did, and some these stories seriously brought tears of gratitude to my eyes. Anyone considering volunteering for SAR or something similar (working at a mountain resort, national park, or similar) should definitely read this first to get a feel for what they might be facing and to understand the mindset required.

☆☆☆☆☆ By Marla Hendrickson

As a person new to the hiking scene here in Utah I never stopped to think just how serious a situation I could find myself in if I didn't make wise choices considering my inexperience and ability. After reading Shaun Roundy's book centered on rescues here locally in Utah and more specifically Utah County I have a much deeper appreciation for my surroundings.

Every chapter is a new experience. Some with happy outcomes and some that are not. I gained a greater appreciation for the skills, dedication and compassion of the men and women of Utah County's Search and Rescue Team who put their lives on the line and life on hold to serve others, all at their own expense.

You will not be able to put the book down. I read it while flying from one destination to another and was disappointed when it was time to land.

What impressed me the most was Shaun's ability to tell a story and include all the details and facts and yet do so very respectfully of the families involved.

Some stories will make you smile and some will make you cry. I have since purchased additionally copies to give to my son a fireman and a good friend who was personally touched by one of the tragedies in the book. You will not regret your purchase.

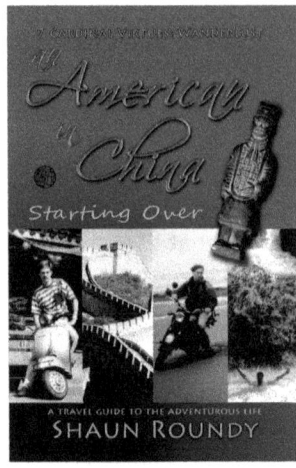

An American in China: Starting Over. A Travel Guide to the Adventurous Life

Order from Amazon.com: bit.ly/chinaguide

A True Story. A Romance. A Travel Guide to the Adventurous Life.

Shaun left in March for a spontaneous six-month voyage through the Orient. Six months later, he didn't return. What did he expect to find by leaving everything behind?

Katie began working her way into Shaun's heart in the weeks before he left, but she couldn't hold him back. Would she ever hold him again?

This true story details a search for the significant questions of life that must precede any meaningful answers. A search through beauty and love and adventure and loss for the wisdom to know when to hold on and when to let go.

Sometimes you must stare into the jaws of death to fully appreciate life. Unwilling to resist the siren song of first-hand experience, Shaun's journey carries him into the salt spray of dangerously high seas, through frothy, typhoon-swollen rivers, and below shattered, crumbling mountainsides that come crashing down around his feet. Passion for living offered no alternatives.

This journey carries him on motorcycles through crowded city streets and wide-open tropical island beaches, on trains rolling for days across the world's most populous country, starting over again and again and again, discovering what it truly means to live, and what living truly costs.

Shaun's engaging writing style will pull you straight into living the adventure yourself. Gather a lifetime of experience in 168 action-packed, heavily illustrated pages.

Sometimes it takes a journey of 20,000 miles to finally arrive at one's own heart. Find your ticket to the journey inside An American in China: starting over.

Reader Reviews:
Great story, great style!
☆☆☆☆☆ By Antone Roundy

The story is moving, entertaining, interesting, exciting... And I love the format: a series of vignettes from the author's experiences in Taiwan and China and reads like a journal of how it all felt, only better than a journal. Every other page includes a photograph (or 2 or 3 or 4...) that really help to communicate the flavor of the people and places you encounter in the book.

☆☆☆☆☆ Nameless Warrior

Generous, interesting, good attempt to slake thirst for the cultural differences and similarities among us. Best to sample life now, will never come around again. Taiwan and Beijing, both worth exploring. A light hearted and hopeful journey. Fresh view from behind another person's eyes. Youth not yet spoiled by bitterness and loss.

Gripping
☆☆☆☆☆ By Trevor

Shaun descriptively reveals his adventure of dropping everything and flying to the other side of the world. For adventure seekers everywhere, this book gives an inside look at experiences that all of us long for. Actually going out and searching for whatever it is that will fill your cup.

Whether it be soul searching, an adventure, freedom from the fast pace life or a longing to break free of the obliviousness to the beauty, mystery and wonderment of the whole world. You'll find, page by page, Shaun does all of this. Paving the way for future wanderlust people wondering if going around the world is really as doable as you've wished it to be.

Break free of monotony and routine. Shaun's style of writing has a natural flow. The book reads like a journal and each randomly sized anecdote is chuck full of details you can tell he is desperate not to forget. It feels like your reading the conversation going on inside his head while he discovers his new world. Coupled with vivid real time context, you feel like you are actually there.

Personally, this books opens new doors and sparks up a brighter flame of wanderlust. This book is a must-read for anyone that has said to themselves, "there's got to be more out there."

Insightful Self-Improvement

The Motivation Equation Workshop
50 Deep Thoughts & Proven Methods for Getting Things Done The Easy Way

Order from Amazon.com:
bit.ly/motequation

Everything you ever wanted is on the other side of action. The way to get there is called Motivation, and it doesn't happen automatically.

Or does it?

Once you understand the most basic principles behind *wanting* to do what you want to get done, you can quit thinking about motivation, because you'll be too busy doing everything.

The Motivation Equation Workshop teaches you how to transform reluctance into eagerness, then adds abundant application exercises to make the lessons personal and turn you into the kind of person who easily gets things done, so you can reach all your goals and enjoy living your fondest dreams.

Love 301: How to Love Yourself
A step-by-step guide to your ideal life experience

Order from Amazon.com:
Paperback: J.mp/self-love-book
Kindle: J.mp/howtoloveyou

After five years of researching the nature of love and designing effective ways to teach it, The University of Love is pleased (and relieved) to present *Love 301: How to*

Love Yourself.
Discover what it means to love yourself and how to implement love's magic into your daily living. Each chapter includes examples, explanations, and several types of application exercises to personalize your learning experience.

True You
The Simple Art of Seeing Who You Really Are

Order from Amazon.com: J.mp/trueyoukindle

If you feel uncomfortable with eye contact, have you ever wondered why? Because it feels intrusive and rude, that's why. It makes you feel exposed and triggers deep insecurities.

But wait – why should simple eye contact makes you feel so vulnerable? Are the eyes truly the window to the soul? Can the secret to your true nature be discovered through those tiny stained-glass portals?

The definitive answer is: Yes! On an intuitive level, you already know that even perfect strangers can see straight through you. Otherwise, why would you mind when they glance at those beautifully colored circles in middle of your face?

The important question is: now that you know, what will you do about it?

True You teaches you step-by-step how to "read" minds and hearts, which may be the simplest yet most life-changing skill you could develop.

It's instructive, nurturing, encouraging and simply fascinating. You'll quickly discover that you are much, much better than you could have guessed.

Heal Your Emotions: A Practical Approach to Speaking your Brain's Languages and Turning Pain into Power.
Order from Amazon.com:
http://bit.ly/healemotions

This easy-to-read 300-page book walks you through hundreds of surprisingly effective ways to quickly develop your intuition and heal anxieties, fears, emotional wounds, limited thinking, and other impediments to living a happy & actualized life.

It also provides dozens of insights to construct a more productive sense of identity and world view.

Reader Reviews:

 By Rislyn on May 28, 2015
Amazingly Helpful! This is my 3rd time though *Heal Your Emotions* and I'm still benefiting every time I pick it up. His techniques are clear, easy to implement, and extremely effective! Whether you want to heal or are working on becoming your best/true self, this book has great things in it to help you!

 By photoatvmom
In the middle of reading this book, and may I just say I LOVE IT! You learn such great techniques and skills to help yourself with anything you are going through.

My personal favorite is an example he gives with a button to release fears, its fantastic! I love all the knowledge I have received especially through understanding your conscious and subconscious. Would recommend to anyone and everyone!

About the Author

Shaun Roundy, MA built the University of Life on the premise that happiness and quality of life depend on behavior, that behavior relies on perspective, and that people generally do the best they know how.

In other words, ideas change lives, and Shaun is determined to change the world for the better. He strives to leave everything better than he found it.

You'll find many engaging and insightful books, articles and podcasts on his favorite life-changing topics, including love, identity, motivation, leadership, meaning and happiness at UofLIFE.com.

Shaun has published twelve books, and taught English at Utah State University and Utah Valley University for fifteen years, and at the Beijing Petroleum University for several months.

He has acted on the Discovery Channel's *Raging Planet*, appeared in the award-winning KUED documentaries *Secrets of the Lost Canyon* and *Search and Rescue*, been interviewed on NPR's *All Things Considered*, along with multiple appearances in local news, which many times became world news.

A college friend once assigned Shaun the personal motto: *"Everything! Now!"*

He has lived on four continents and one tropical island, speaks several languages, has volunteered on his county's active search and rescue team for nearly 20 years, and chaired the Mountain Rescue Association's Intermountain Region for over half that time.

He has climbed 18,000-foot mountains, rappelled thousand-foot waterfalls, paddled alone for 120 miles of ocean and everglades, backpacked through Asia, sailed 2,500 miles through two oceans, rides motorcycles, rock climbs, backpacks, skis, SCUBA dives, and much more.

www.ingramcontent.com/pod-product-compliance
Lightning Source LLC
Chambersburg PA
CBHW071519040426
42444CB00008B/1711